THE WORD BECAME FLESH AND
MADE HIS DWELLING AMONG US.
WE HAVE SEEN HIS GLORY,
THE GLORY OF THE ONE AND ONLY,
WHO CAME FROM THE FATHER,
FULL OF GRACE AND TRUTH.

JOHN 1:14

presented:

to: _____

_____

by: _____

_____

on: _____

D0883496

_____

the
family
reading
Bible

christmas
story

the
family
reading
Bible

christmas
story

ZONDERVAN®

The Christmas Story
Copyright © 2010 by Zondervan

The Holy Bible, *New International Version*®
Copyright © 1973, 1978, 1984 by Biblica, Inc.™
All rights reserved

Published by Zondervan
Grand Rapids, Michigan 49530, *U.S.A.*

www.zondervan.com

Library of Congress Catalog Card Number 2010930452

table of contents

If you would like to read the stories of Jesus' birth and the shepherds and angels on Christmas Eve and Christmas Day, begin the first reading of *The Christmas Story*, "David's Forever Kingdom," on December 13 and read one chapter each day.

how to use
The Christmas Story

Families matter to God. Your family matters to God. He wants your family to be a safe, loving haven in which you can raise your children to love and obey him and believe in his Son, Jesus.

God gives you, the parent, the awesome job of teaching your children about him and his Word. The Bible clearly instructs you to teach God's commands to your children:

> Hear, O Israel: The LORD our God, the LORD is one. Love the LORD your God with all your heart and with all your soul and with all your strength. These commandments that I give you today are to be upon your hearts. Impress them on your children. Talk about them when you sit at home and when you walk along the road, when you lie down and when you get up.
> —Deuteronomy 6:4–9

The Christmas Story, adapted from *The Family Reading Bible,* will help you lead your children in devotions through the Christmas season. Twenty readings span the "big picture" of God's grace in sending Jesus, our Savior to live on earth and walk among us. There are seven readings from the Old Testament that cover the prophecies and some background about the Messiah's coming. The next eight stories relate the events immediately surrounding and including Jesus' birth. The final six readings show how Jesus is the Son of God and how Jesus has made God's love and forgiveness available to every one of us. As a result, you and your family will follow and understand the story of Jesus' birth as you never have before.

Each reading also includes excerpts from the New International Version, engaging questions and points of interest that will help you and your family connect with the Christmas story in a fresh way.

Explanation of Features
Included With Each Reading

Just the Facts are straight-forward questions with concrete answers. A verse reference follows each question so you can easily find the specific answer. Some of the questions are designed to be easily answered by younger children; some are harder to provide a challenge to older children.

Let's Talk questions are intended to encourage discussion. There may more than one "right" answer. Some are open-ended and have no answer. These questions are not necessarily connected to a particular verse. Use the Let's Talk questions to encourage your children to think about what God wants you to learn from the story that's been read. Some of these questions may be too difficult for young children. Feel free to skip them if you wish.

Why This Matters underscores the core message of the passage and will help you answer the question that kids often ask: "Why do I need to know this?"

Points of Interest highlight something surprising or little known about the passage. This might be a cultural insight, a geographic or archaeological fact, a historical note or a fun detail. From time to time it may explain a puzzling aspect of the passage.

Tips for Parents

- Do the best you can to have devotions regularly with your family, but don't feel guilty if you miss sometimes. With today's busy schedules, many families find it difficult to have a family devotional time every day.

- Every family is different. You may find that a slightly different structure to your devotional time than that suggested here works best for you. Feel free to adapt this information to the needs of your family.

- We hope that you and your family are richly blessed by reading and experiencing God's Word through this book.

a brief history of God's people

The Bible tells many stories about the history of God's people. If you'd like to know more about these stories, you can find them in the *Family Reading Bible*. Check it out! In the meantime, here is an overview to give you some background for *The Christmas Story* from the *Family Reading Bible*.

Long, long ago God told a man named Abram (later called Abraham) to travel to a new country. He didn't tell Abraham why or where he was supposed to go, but Abraham had faith in God, so he packed and went. After Abraham had traveled a long way, God brought him to the land that would become his own. God told Abraham that he would make his family great and that his descendants would be as numerous as the sand on the seashore. To prove it, God told Abraham that he and his wife, Sarah, would have a son. They were old and it seemed impossible, but Sarah got pregnant, and their son, Isaac, was born.

When Isaac grew up, he married Rebekah, and they had a son named Jacob. When Jacob, who was also called Israel, grew up, he had 12 sons, and his sons each had large families. God was faithful to this family. He took care of them and remembered the promises he had made to Abraham.

Because of a famine, Jacob and his sons and their families and animals went to live in Egypt. Over time, they had more children and their families grew very large. Because Jacob's descendants, now called the Israelites, were so many, the Egyptians became afraid of them and made them their slaves. Jacob's descendants served in Egypt for many years, and they had to work very hard. How they suffered! They asked God to get them out of Egypt and out of slavery, so God sent a man named Moses to help them. God sent plague after plague to convince the king of Egypt to free the Israelites. Finally a day came when the king told Moses, "Leave my people, you and the Israelites! Go ... Take your flocks and herds, as you have said, and go" (Exodus 12:31–32).

Moses led the Israelites on a journey out of Egypt and to the land God had promised to their ancestor Abraham. Sometimes they obeyed God on the journey, but sometimes they didn't. When they disobeyed, God disciplined his people. Because the Israelites disobeyed God, they wandered in the desert for 40 years. Still, God did not forget them; he provided water and food for them.

After Moses died, another leader, Joshua, led the people into the land God had promised them. There, each tribe was given land of its own. God gave the Israelites many laws and commandments for living holy lives that would be pleasing to him. Sometimes the people didn't do what God asked (that is called sin). God appointed Levites, members of one of the Israelite tribes, to serve him and to make sure the people worshiped him correctly and reverently. Some of the Levites were appointed as priests. Because of the Israelites' sins, the priests offered animal sacrifices to God so they could be right with God once again. But the people kept sinning, so the sacrifices had to be made over and over again.

God loved his people and wanted the very best for them. But to be blessed by their holy God, they had to live holy lives and follow God's rules. God wanted to be number one in their lives, but the people were often tempted to worship false gods. When they fell away from God, he sent leaders called judges to get them out of trouble. The judges told the people what God wanted them to do.

Often the judges were military leaders who led the Israelites to victory over their enemies.

Because the nations all around the Israelites had kings, the Israelites wanted a king too. God warned them that it wouldn't work out well for them, but they insisted. God appointed a king named Saul. But Saul decided to do things his own way, so God took away Saul's power and made a shepherd boy, David, the son of Jesse, Israel's king. David, though he wasn't perfect, had a heart for God. Through David, God continued to keep the promise he had made to Abraham. And that's where the story of Christmas begins.

David's Forever Kingdom

King David loved God and wanted to build a temple for God to live in. But God said he would establish an even greater "house" — a kingdom that would last forever. God had great plans for David's family. Not just for his son or grandson, but for someone who would be born many generations later.

2 Samuel 7:1-17

God's Promise to David

7 After the king was settled in his palace and the LORD had given him rest from all his enemies around him, ²he said to Nathan the prophet, "Here I am, living in a palace of cedar, while the ark of God remains in a tent."

³Nathan replied to the king, "Whatever you have in mind, go ahead and do it, for the LORD is with you."

⁴That night the word of the LORD came to Nathan, saying:

⁵"Go and tell my servant David, 'This is what the LORD says: Are you the one to build me a house to dwell in? ⁶I have not dwelt in a house from the day I brought the Israelites up out of Egypt to this day. I have been moving from place to place with a tent as my dwelling. ⁷Wherever I have moved with all the Israelites, did I ever say to any of their rulers whom I commanded to shepherd my people Israel, "Why have you not built me a house of cedar?"'

[8]"Now then, tell my servant David, 'This is what the LORD Almighty says: I took you from the pasture and from following the flock to be ruler over my people Israel. [9]I have been with you wherever you have gone, and I have cut off all your enemies from before you. Now I will make your name great, like the names of the greatest men of the earth. [10]And I will provide a place for my people Israel and will plant them so that they can have a home of their own and no longer be disturbed. Wicked people will not oppress them anymore, as they did at the beginning [11]and have done ever since the time I appointed leaders[a] over my people Israel. I will also give you rest from all your enemies.

"'The LORD declares to you that the LORD himself will establish a house for you: [12]When your days are over and you rest with your fathers, I will raise up your offspring to succeed you, who will come from your own body, and I will establish his kingdom. [13]He is the one who will build a house for my Name, and I will establish the throne of his kingdom forever. [14]I will be his father, and he will be my son. When he does wrong, I will punish him with the rod of men, with floggings inflicted by men. [15]But my love will never be taken away from him, as I took it away from Saul, whom I removed from before you. [16]Your house and your kingdom will endure forever before me[b]; your throne will be established forever.'"

[17]Nathan reported to David all the words of this entire revelation.

---

[a] 11 Traditionally *judges*   [b] 16 Some Hebrew manuscripts and Septuagint; most Hebrew manuscripts *you*

JUST THE FACTS

1. Who gave God's message to King David? (v. 4)
2. What did God promise his people? (vv. 10–11)
3. What did God promise David and his descendants? (vv. 12,15–16)

LET'S TALK

1. What do you think it meant in David's time to "establish a house"? In what ways are families important in our culture today? How is your family important to you?
2. Who were your ancestors? How many generations can you identify? What is it like to imagine having children and grandchildren who will come after you?

WHY THIS MATTERS

God made a promise to David that he would establish a kingdom for David's descendants. Hundreds of years after David died, God sent his Son, Jesus, who came from David's family, to be the king of the Jews.

POINTS OF INTEREST

7:6 The "tent" God was referring to was the tabernacle that had been his portable dwelling place ever since the Israelites camped at Mount Sinai in the desert. It was intended to be used only while the Israelites were on the march. But the Israelites had lived in the land God had promised them for more than 400 years and still had not built a permanent temple — a house in which they could worship the one true God.

The Sign of Immanuel

Years after God made the kingdom of Israel great through King David, God's people were again disobedient to his laws and commandments. The nation of Israel became divided into two: one country was called Israel and the other was called Judah. So God sent messengers, called prophets, to announce his words to the people. Isaiah gave this prophecy first to King Ahaz of Judah when his country was about to be invaded by the armies of Israel and Aram. The king was fearful; he was not trusting God to take care of him and his country. The prophecy was fulfilled a short time later when a young woman, who may have been Isaiah's wife, became pregnant (see Isaiah 8:3–10). But the prophecy was also fulfilled much later when another young woman, Mary, became pregnant (see Luke 1:26–38).

Isaiah 7:10—8:10

[10] Again the LORD spoke to Ahaz, [11] "Ask the LORD your God for a sign, whether in the deepest depths or in the highest heights."

[12] But Ahaz said, "I will not ask; I will not put the LORD to the test."

[13] Then Isaiah said, "Hear now, you house of David! Is it not enough to try the patience of men? Will you try the patience of my God also? [14] Therefore the Lord himself will give you[a] a sign: The virgin will be

[a] *14* The Hebrew is plural.

with child and will give birth to a son, and[a] will call him Immanuel.[b] [15]He will eat curds and honey when he knows enough to reject the wrong and choose the right. [16]But before the boy knows enough to reject the wrong and choose the right, the land of the two kings you dread will be laid waste. [17]The LORD will bring on you and on your people and on the house of your father a time unlike any since Ephraim broke away from Judah—he will bring the king of Assyria."

[18]In that day the LORD will whistle for flies from the distant streams of Egypt and for bees from the land of Assyria. [19]They will all come and settle in the steep ravines and in the crevices in the rocks, on all the thornbushes and at all the water holes. [20]In that day the Lord will use a razor hired from beyond the River[c]—the king of Assyria—to shave your head and the hair of your legs, and to take off your beards also. [21]In that day, a man will keep alive a young cow and two goats. [22]And because of the abundance of the milk they give, he will have curds to eat. All who remain in the land will eat curds and honey. [23]In that day, in every place where there were a thousand vines worth a thousand silver shekels,[d] there will be only briers and thorns. [24]Men will go there with bow and arrow, for the land will be covered with briers and thorns. [25]As for all the hills once cultivated by the hoe, you will no longer go there for fear of the briers and thorns; they will become places where cattle are turned loose and where sheep run.

Assyria, the LORD's Instrument

8 The LORD said to me, "Take a large scroll and write on it with an ordinary pen: Maher-Shalal-Hash-

---

[a] *14* Masoretic Text; Dead Sea Scrolls *and he* or *and they*
[b] *14* *Immanuel* means *God with us.*   [c] *20* That is, the Euphrates
[d] *23* That is, about 25 pounds (about 11.5 kilograms)

Baz.[a] [2]And I will call in Uriah the priest and Zechariah son of Jeberekiah as reliable witnesses for me."

[3]Then I went to the prophetess, and she conceived and gave birth to a son. And the LORD said to me, "Name him Maher-Shalal-Hash-Baz. [4]Before the boy knows how to say 'My father' or 'My mother,' the wealth of Damascus and the plunder of Samaria will be carried off by the king of Assyria."

[5]The LORD spoke to me again:

[6]"Because this people has rejected
    the gently flowing waters of Shiloah
and rejoices over Rezin
    and the son of Remaliah,
[7]therefore the Lord is about to bring against them
    the mighty floodwaters of the River[b]—
the king of Assyria with all his pomp.
It will overflow all its channels,
    run over all its banks
[8]and sweep on into Judah, swirling over it,
    passing through it and reaching up to the
        neck.
Its outspread wings will cover the breadth of
        your land,
    O Immanuel[c]!"

[9]Raise the war cry,[d] you nations, and be shattered!
    Listen, all you distant lands.
Prepare for battle, and be shattered!
    Prepare for battle, and be shattered!
[10]Devise your strategy, but it will be thwarted;
    propose your plan, but it will not stand,
for God is with us.[e]

---

[a] *1 Maher-Shalal-Hash-Baz* means *quick to the plunder, swift to the spoil*; also in verse 3.   [b] 7 That is, the Euphrates
[c] *8 Immanuel* means *God with us.*   [d] *9* Or *Do your worst*
[e] *10* Hebrew *Immanuel*

JUST THE FACTS

1. What did God want Ahaz to do? (7:11)
2. What was the sign God promised to send? (7:14)
3. What was the boy going to eat? (7:15)

LET'S TALK

1. This prophecy was meant for Ahaz's time, but it was also a foreshadowing of Jesus' coming. Why do you think the prophet gave two meanings to these verses?
2. "Immanuel" (7:14) means "God with us. " When do we use the name "Immanuel" today? Can you think of a song about Immanuel?

WHY THIS MATTERS

The sign God gave to Ahaz — a virgin giving birth to a son and naming him Immanuel — is a key promise about the coming of Jesus Christ. When Jesus came to earth, God really *was* with us.

POINTS OF INTEREST

7:15 The land was devastated by the Assyrians, so there was no harvest. The people lived on anything they could find on the land. What they found was curds and honey; these two items refer to a simple diet of natural foods. Curds were a kind of yogurt.

A Child Is Born

This passage is another part of the prophecy Isaiah gave to Ahaz, the king of Judah. The Assyrian Empire was threatening to take over the lands that surrounded it. Isaiah warned the people about the destruction that was to come to Judah. God's nation, it appeared, would be torn down, but it would not be dead forever. Isaiah's prophecy is not only about his own time but also about a time far in the future.

Isaiah 9:1–7

To Us a Child Is Born

9 Nevertheless, there will be no more gloom for those who were in distress. In the past he humbled the land of Zebulun and the land of Naphtali, but in the future he will honor Galilee of the Gentiles, by the way of the sea, along the Jordan—

²The people walking in darkness
    have seen a great light;
on those living in the land of the shadow of death[a]
    a light has dawned.
³You have enlarged the nation
    and increased their joy;
they rejoice before you
    as people rejoice at the harvest,
as men rejoice
    when dividing the plunder.

[a] 2 Or *land of darkness*

⁴For as in the day of Midian's defeat,
    you have shattered
the yoke that burdens them,
    the bar across their shoulders,
    the rod of their oppressor.
⁵Every warrior's boot used in battle
    and every garment rolled in blood
will be destined for burning,
    will be fuel for the fire.
⁶For to us a child is born,
    to us a son is given,
    and the government will be on his shoulders.
And he will be called
    Wonderful Counselor,ᵃ Mighty God,
    Everlasting Father, Prince of Peace.
⁷Of the increase of his government and peace
    there will be no end.
He will reign on David's throne
    and over his kingdom,
establishing and upholding it
    with justice and righteousness
    from that time on and forever.
The zeal of the LORD Almighty
    will accomplish this.

ᵃ 6 Or *Wonderful, Counselor*

1. What event was coming? (v. 6)
2. What are some of the names this special child would have? (v. 6)
3. How long would this king reign? (v. 7)

LET'S TALK

1. What is it like when everything is dark? What about when someone turns on a light? How does this news bring people out of "darkness" and into "light" (v. 2)?
2. This child would have several names. What does each of them mean to you? Discuss each one.

WHY THIS MATTERS

Though God's people were facing a frightening enemy, God did not let them face the enemy without a message of hope for a glorious future — a time when they would live in peace, prosperity and joy.

POINTS OF INTEREST

9:1 The land of the tribes of Zebulun and Naphtali became the land of Galilee. When Jesus began his public ministry in Galilee, he fulfilled Isaiah's prophecy recorded in verses 1–2.

God's People Ask for Salvation

This psalm, or song, was written as a prayer to God when the nation of Israel was torn apart by a foreign nation, probably Assyria. God's people had to flee from their homes and farms. They suffered many hardships. They longed for God to send someone to save them from their enemies and restore their nation. At this time, God's people described the nation as a vine that had been planted but had now been trampled and burned.

Psalm 80:1–19

Psalm 80

For the director of music. To ˌthe tune ofˌ
"The Lilies of the Covenant." Of Asaph. A psalm.

¹ Hear us, O Shepherd of Israel,
    you who lead Joseph like a flock;
you who sit enthroned between the cherubim,
        shine forth
²   before Ephraim, Benjamin and Manasseh.
Awaken your might;
    come and save us.

³ Restore us, O God;
    make your face shine upon us,
    that we may be saved.

⁴ O Lord God Almighty,
    how long will your anger smolder
    against the prayers of your people?

⁵You have fed them with the bread of tears;
    you have made them drink tears by the
        bowlful.
⁶You have made us a source of contention to our
        neighbors,
    and our enemies mock us.

⁷Restore us, O God Almighty;
    make your face shine upon us,
    that we may be saved.

⁸You brought a vine out of Egypt;
    you drove out the nations and planted it.
⁹You cleared the ground for it,
    and it took root and filled the land.
¹⁰The mountains were covered with its shade,
    the mighty cedars with its branches.
¹¹It sent out its boughs to the Sea,ᵃ
    its shoots as far as the River.ᵇ

¹²Why have you broken down its walls
    so that all who pass by pick its grapes?
¹³Boars from the forest ravage it
    and the creatures of the field feed on it.
¹⁴Return to us, O God Almighty!
    Look down from heaven and see!
  Watch over this vine,
¹⁵   the root your right hand has planted,
    the sonᶜ you have raised up for yourself.

¹⁶Your vine is cut down, it is burned with fire;
    at your rebuke your people perish.
¹⁷Let your hand rest on the man at your right
        hand,
    the son of man you have raised up for
        yourself.

ᵃ 11 Probably the Mediterranean   ᵇ 11 That is, the Euphrates
ᶜ 15 Or *branch*

¹⁸Then we will not turn away from you;
  revive us, and we will call on your name.

¹⁹Restore us, O LORD God Almighty;
  make your face shine upon us,
  that we may be saved.

JUST THE FACTS

1. Where does God sit? (v. 1)
2. What did this writer ask for? (vv. 2–3)
3. What happened to the vine? (vv. 8–11,16)

LET'S TALK

1. Why do you think the writer used the word picture of a vine? Why not just say "Israel"?
2. What did the people promise to do if God sent them a ruler? (v. 18) What did they mean by saying they would call on God's name and not turn away?

WHY THIS MATTERS

God's people continued to plead with God to show mercy and save them. He answered this plea many centuries later by sending his Son, Jesus.

POINTS OF INTEREST

80:1 Cherubim are a special kind of angel. They were guardians protecting the way to the tree of life in the Garden of Eden. They also protected the ark of the covenant in the tabernacle and in the temple. In this psalm they are said to guard God's heavenly throne. Cherubim are described as having wings and a combination of human and animal characteristics.

The Branch From Jesse

Sometimes after a tree is cut down, a new green shoot grows out of the stump. Jesse was King David's father, so the "stump of Jesse" (Isaiah 1:1) was Isaiah's way of referring to David's family. When the nation of Israel was divided and eventually destroyed, it appeared that David's family had died out. But God promised that a "shoot" would grow from it — a new leader would be born to give the nation hope.

Isaiah 11:1-10

The Branch From Jesse

11 A shoot will come up from the stump of Jesse;

from his roots a Branch will bear fruit.
²The Spirit of the LORD will rest on him—
the Spirit of wisdom and of understanding,
the Spirit of counsel and of power,
the Spirit of knowledge and of the fear of the LORD—
³and he will delight in the fear of the LORD.

He will not judge by what he sees with his eyes,
or decide by what he hears with his ears;
⁴but with righteousness he will judge the needy,
with justice he will give decisions for the poor of the earth.
He will strike the earth with the rod of his mouth;

with the breath of his lips he will slay the
  wicked.
⁵Righteousness will be his belt
  and faithfulness the sash around his waist.

⁶The wolf will live with the lamb,
  the leopard will lie down with the goat,
 the calf and the lion and the yearling^a together;
  and a little child will lead them.
⁷The cow will feed with the bear,
  their young will lie down together,
  and the lion will eat straw like the ox.
⁸The infant will play near the hole of the cobra,
  and the young child put his hand into the
    viper's nest.
⁹They will neither harm nor destroy
  on all my holy mountain,
 for the earth will be full of the knowledge of the
  LORD
  as the waters cover the sea.

¹⁰In that day the Root of Jesse will stand as a banner
for the peoples; the nations will rally to him, and his
place of rest will be glorious.

ᵃ 6 Hebrew; Septuagint *lion will feed*

1. What gifts would the Spirit give this "shoot" (v. 1) when the Spirit rested on him? (v. 2)

2. What would the "shoot" wear as his belt? As his sash? (v. 5)

3. What animals are mentioned in this reading? How will these animals someday behave? (vv. 6–9)

LET'S TALK

1. Why do you think Isaiah talked about the Messiah's coming by using words about growing things, like the "Branch" and the "shoot" (v. 1)? What sometimes happens when you cut off a plant that still has deep, living roots?

2. What did Isaiah mean when he said, "The wolf will live with the lamb, the leopard will lie down with the goat" (v. 6)? What would life be like if the world was that peaceful?

WHY THIS MATTERS

God gave his people hope. He taught them to look for the Messiah by telling them what he was going to do long before it happened. Just as Israel looked for the Messiah, we can hope and look forward to Jesus coming again to bring a time when there will be no more violence or cruelty.

POINTS OF INTEREST

11:8 The cobra and the viper are poisonous snakes. The cobra, which can grow to eight and a half feet long, was the deadly Egyptian cobra, used in Egypt as a religious symbol. It is usually found on the north and east coasts of Africa, with a variation of the species located in the Arabian Desert. The picture of a child calmly playing near these feared reptiles was a sure sign that the Messiah would change everything.

God Will Come to Save

In another prophecy Isaiah said that the coming Messiah would heal people and perform other miracles. When Jesus came, he did all the things that Isaiah had talked about hundreds of years before.

Isaiah 35:1–10

Joy of the Redeemed

35 The desert and the parched land will be glad;
  the wilderness will rejoice and blossom.
Like the crocus, [2]it will burst into bloom;
  it will rejoice greatly and shout for joy.
The glory of Lebanon will be given to it,
  the splendor of Carmel and Sharon;
they will see the glory of the LORD,
  the splendor of our God.

[3]Strengthen the feeble hands,
  steady the knees that give way;
[4]say to those with fearful hearts,
  "Be strong, do not fear;
your God will come,
  he will come with vengeance;
with divine retribution
  he will come to save you."

[5]Then will the eyes of the blind be opened
  and the ears of the deaf unstopped.
[6]Then will the lame leap like a deer,
  and the mute tongue shout for joy.

Water will gush forth in the wilderness
and streams in the desert.
⁷The burning sand will become a pool,
the thirsty ground bubbling springs.
In the haunts where jackals once lay,
grass and reeds and papyrus will grow.

⁸And a highway will be there;
it will be called the Way of Holiness.
The unclean will not journey on it;
it will be for those who walk in that Way;
wicked fools will not go about on it.ᵃ
⁹No lion will be there,
nor will any ferocious beast get up on it;
they will not be found there.
But only the redeemed will walk there,
¹⁰ and the ransomed of the LORD will return.
They will enter Zion with singing;
everlasting joy will crown their heads.
Gladness and joy will overtake them,
and sorrow and sighing will flee away.

ᵃ 8 Or / *the simple will not stray from it*

JUST THE FACTS

1. How would the desert and wilderness rejoice? (vv. 1–2)

2. What would happen to blind people? Deaf people? Lame people? (vv. 5–6)

3. What would be the name of the highway? (v. 8)

LET'S TALK

1. A "contrast" shows the differences between two things, such as the contrast between desert land and land that has plenty of rainfall. How many contrasts can you find in this passage?

2. Who will walk on the Way of Holiness? How do you picture this? What will it be like?

WHY THIS MATTERS

God promised that the Messiah's coming would change people in many ways. The Messiah would heal, perform miracles and bring salvation to everyone who believed in him. When Jesus the Messiah came, he brought a new kingdom into being.

POINTS OF INTEREST

35:1 The crocus mentioned here is not the early spring flower that we are familiar with. Rather it refers to the saffron crocus, a spring flowering herb used to produce saffron powder, which is used in cooking. This flower is fairly common in Palestine today.

The Messiah Will Come From Bethlehem

God gave Micah a message for the people of Israel: in their lifetime their nation would be destroyed. But God also gave Micah a vision of bright hope — with details! Micah predicted an important event in a little town in Judah that would make the town famous.

Micah 5:1-5

A Promised Ruler From Bethlehem

5 Marshal your troops, O city of troops,[a]
   for a siege is laid against us.
They will strike Israel's ruler
   on the cheek with a rod.

[2] "But you, Bethlehem Ephrathah,
   though you are small among the clans[b] of Judah,
out of you will come for me
   one who will be ruler over Israel,
whose origins[c] are from of old,
   from ancient times.[d]"

[3] Therefore Israel will be abandoned
   until the time when she who is in labor gives
      birth
and the rest of his brothers return
   to join the Israelites.

[a] 1 Or *Strengthen your walls, O walled city*   [b] 2 Or *rulers*
[c] 2 Hebrew *goings out*   [d] 2 Or *from days of eternity*

⁴He will stand and shepherd his flock
    in the strength of the LORD,
      in the majesty of the name of the LORD his
        God.
And they will live securely, for then his greatness
    will reach to the ends of the earth.
⁵ And he will be their peace.

Deliverance and Destruction

When the Assyrian invades our land
    and marches through our fortresses,
we will raise against him seven shepherds,
    even eight leaders of men.

JUST THE FACTS

1. What town was the prophet talking about? (v. 2)
2. What did the prophet say about this small town? (v. 2)
3. What would this ruler be like? (vv. 4–5)

LET'S TALK

1. What do you think it means that the ruler over Israel would be one "whose origins are from of old, from ancient times" (v. 2)?
2. How has Jesus' greatness reached to the ends of the earth? Discuss.

WHY THIS MATTERS

Christ existed long before history began. He was present at the creation of the world. Jesus will rule forever as our shepherd, giving us peace and security as our "Prince of Peace" (Isaiah 9:6). God chose the little town of Bethlehem to be Jesus' birthplace long before he was born.

POINTS OF INTEREST

5:2 Though Bethlehem was a small town, it had an important place in the history of God's people. Jacob buried his wife Rachel there (when it was called Ephrath, see Genesis 35:19). Ibzan, a judge of Israel, was from this town. So were Boaz, the husband of Ruth, and David, who kept his father's sheep and was anointed king by Samuel. Modern Bethlehem is a small village of fewer than 10,000 people. The surrounding hillsides abound in figs, almonds, olives and grape vines. The shepherds' fields are located northeast of the town still today.

The Birth of John Foretold

Many years later, Israel came under the powerful rule of the Roman Empire. The empire ruled over the Jews and made them pay heavy taxes. They still longed for a savior to rescue them and restore their nation. The right time came for God to fulfill his promise and send the Messiah. But first he would send a special messenger to announce Jesus' coming and get the people ready to accept their Savior.

Luke 1:5-25

The Birth of John the Baptist Foretold

⁵In the time of Herod king of Judea there was a priest named Zechariah, who belonged to the priestly division of Abijah; his wife Elizabeth was also a descendant of Aaron. ⁶Both of them were upright in the sight of God, observing all the Lord's commandments and regulations blamelessly. ⁷But they had no children, because Elizabeth was barren; and they were both well along in years.

⁸Once when Zechariah's division was on duty and he was serving as priest before God, ⁹he was chosen by lot, according to the custom of the priesthood, to go into the temple of the Lord and burn incense. ¹⁰And when the time for the burning of incense came, all the assembled worshipers were praying outside.

¹¹Then an angel of the Lord appeared to him, standing at the right side of the altar of incense. ¹²When Zechariah saw him, he was startled and was gripped

with fear. ¹³But the angel said to him: "Do not be afraid, Zechariah; your prayer has been heard. Your wife Elizabeth will bear you a son, and you are to give him the name John. ¹⁴He will be a joy and delight to you, and many will rejoice because of his birth, ¹⁵for he will be great in the sight of the Lord. He is never to take wine or other fermented drink, and he will be filled with the Holy Spirit even from birth.ᵃ ¹⁶Many of the people of Israel will he bring back to the Lord their God. ¹⁷And he will go on before the Lord, in the spirit and power of Elijah, to turn the hearts of the fathers to their children and the disobedient to the wisdom of the righteous—to make ready a people prepared for the Lord."

¹⁸Zechariah asked the angel, "How can I be sure of this? I am an old man and my wife is well along in years."

¹⁹The angel answered, "I am Gabriel. I stand in the presence of God, and I have been sent to speak to you and to tell you this good news. ²⁰And now you will be silent and not able to speak until the day this happens, because you did not believe my words, which will come true at their proper time."

²¹Meanwhile, the people were waiting for Zechariah and wondering why he stayed so long in the temple. ²²When he came out, he could not speak to them. They realized he had seen a vision in the temple, for he kept making signs to them but remained unable to speak.

²³When his time of service was completed, he returned home. ²⁴After this his wife Elizabeth became pregnant and for five months remained in seclusion. ²⁵"The Lord has done this for me," she said. "In these days he has shown his favor and taken away my disgrace among the people."

ᵃ 15 Or *from his mother's womb*

1. Who was Zechariah? What was his wife's name? (v. 5)

2. Who visited Zechariah in the temple? What was the message? (vv. 11–17)

3. What happened to Zechariah? Why? (v. 20)

LET'S TALK

1. Was Zechariah's inability to speak a punishment or a blessing? Explain.

2. In what way would John "go on before the Lord, in the spirit and power of Elijah" (v. 17)? Why did the angel compare John to the Old Testament prophet?

WHY THIS MATTERS

God kept the promise he had made to his people through the prophet Isaiah. John was "a voice of one calling: 'In the desert prepare the way for the LORD'" (Isaiah 40:3). John preached repentance so the people could accept the Good News of Jesus.

POINTS OF INTEREST

1:5 Both Zechariah and Elizabeth were Levites and descendants of Aaron. Only men from the family line of Aaron could be priests. Groups of priests rotated serving in the temple. They presented sacrifices and offerings to God, taught and carried out God's laws for worship, maintained the temple, lit lamps and burned incense, and talked to God on behalf of the people of Israel. Zechariah was on duty and serving as priest when the angel came to him in the temple.

An Angel Announces Jesus' Birth

When Zechariah's wife Elizabeth was six months pregnant, her young cousin Mary had a very special visitor. An angel told Mary that she had been chosen to give birth to a special child, the Son of the Most High. Mary was betrothed (engaged) to a man named Joseph, who was from the family line of David.

Luke 1:26–56

The Birth of Jesus Foretold

[26] In the sixth month, God sent the angel Gabriel to Nazareth, a town in Galilee, [27] to a virgin pledged to be married to a man named Joseph, a descendant of David. The virgin's name was Mary. [28] The angel went to her and said, "Greetings, you who are highly favored! The Lord is with you."

[29] Mary was greatly troubled at his words and wondered what kind of greeting this might be. [30] But the angel said to her, "Do not be afraid, Mary, you have found favor with God. [31] You will be with child and give birth to a son, and you are to give him the name Jesus. [32] He will be great and will be called the Son of the Most High. The Lord God will give him the throne of his father David, [33] and he will reign over the house of Jacob forever; his kingdom will never end."

[34] "How will this be," Mary asked the angel, "since I am a virgin?"

[35] The angel answered, "The Holy Spirit will come upon you, and the power of the Most High will

49

overshadow you. So the holy one to be born will be called[a] the Son of God. 36 Even Elizabeth your relative is going to have a child in her old age, and she who was said to be barren is in her sixth month. 37 For nothing is impossible with God."

38 "I am the Lord's servant," Mary answered. "May it be to me as you have said." Then the angel left her.

Mary Visits Elizabeth

39 At that time Mary got ready and hurried to a town in the hill country of Judea, 40 where she entered Zechariah's home and greeted Elizabeth. 41 When Elizabeth heard Mary's greeting, the baby leaped in her womb, and Elizabeth was filled with the Holy Spirit. 42 In a loud voice she exclaimed: "Blessed are you among women, and blessed is the child you will bear! 43 But why am I so favored, that the mother of my Lord should come to me? 44 As soon as the sound of your greeting reached my ears, the baby in my womb leaped for joy. 45 Blessed is she who has believed that what the Lord has said to her will be accomplished!"

Mary's Song

46 And Mary said:

"My soul glorifies the Lord
47   and my spirit rejoices in God my Savior,
48 for he has been mindful
       of the humble state of his servant.
   From now on all generations will call me blessed,
49   for the Mighty One has done great things for
            me—
       holy is his name.
50 His mercy extends to those who fear him,
       from generation to generation.

---

[a] 35 Or *So the child to be born will be called holy,*

⁵¹ He has performed mighty deeds with his arm;
he has scattered those who are proud in their
inmost thoughts.
⁵² He has brought down rulers from their thrones
but has lifted up the humble.
⁵³ He has filled the hungry with good things
but has sent the rich away empty.
⁵⁴ He has helped his servant Israel,
remembering to be merciful
⁵⁵ to Abraham and his descendants forever,
even as he said to our fathers."

⁵⁶ Mary stayed with Elizabeth for about three months
and then returned home.

JUST THE FACTS

1. What was the name of the angel who visited Mary? (v. 26)

2. What was the name Mary was to give her child? (v. 31)

3. What was Mary's final answer to the angel? (v. 38)

LET'S TALK

1. Why did Mary believe this very unusual announcement? Why did Mary visit Elizabeth?

2. What was Mary like? Why do you think God chose her to be Jesus' mother?

WHY THIS MATTERS

God showed that he can do the impossible — a virgin became pregnant by his Holy Spirit, and God's Son came into the world. Mary's song of praise in Luke 1:46–55 tells how wonderful this news is.

POINTS OF INTEREST

1:39–40 Mary's home in Nazareth was about 65 miles away from Jerusalem, where her cousin Elizabeth lived. In Bible times, that distance would have taken several days to travel. It was common for relatives to visit and stay for months at a time, like Mary did.

Joseph Has a Dream

Mary was promised to be married to Joseph. In those days betrothal, or engagement, was a very important legal agreement. But when Mary told Joseph she was pregnant, Joseph no longer wanted to marry her. Then he had a dream that convinced him that everything that had happened was from the Holy Spirit of God.

Matthew 1:18–25

The Birth of Jesus Christ

¹⁸This is how the birth of Jesus Christ came about: His mother Mary was pledged to be married to Joseph, but before they came together, she was found to be with child through the Holy Spirit. ¹⁹Because Joseph her husband was a righteous man and did not want to expose her to public disgrace, he had in mind to divorce her quietly.

²⁰But after he had considered this, an angel of the Lord appeared to him in a dream and said, "Joseph son of David, do not be afraid to take Mary home as your wife, because what is conceived in her is from the Holy Spirit. ²¹She will give birth to a son, and you are to give him the name Jesus,[a] because he will save his people from their sins."

²²All this took place to fulfill what the Lord had said through the prophet: ²³"The virgin will be with

[a] 21 Jesus is the Greek form of Joshua, which means the LORD saves.

child and will give birth to a son, and they will call him Immanuel"[a]—which means, "God with us."

[24]When Joseph woke up, he did what the angel of the Lord had commanded him and took Mary home as his wife. [25]But he had no union with her until she gave birth to a son. And he gave him the name Jesus.

[a] *23* Isaiah 7:14

JUST THE FACTS

1. Who talked to Joseph in a dream? What did the messenger call Joseph? (v. 20)

2. What did the messenger tell Joseph would happen? (v. 21)

3. What was Joseph told to name the baby? Why? (v. 21)

LET'S TALK

1. How do you think Joseph felt after his dream? Have you ever had a dream that made you feel better about a situation?

2. Why is it important that these events took place according to the prophecy in verse 23?

WHY THIS MATTERS

God wanted Jesus, his own Son, to have both a father and a mother to care for him and bring him up according to the Law of Moses and the law of the land. God worked everything out to fulfill every detail prophesied by the prophets.

POINTS OF INTEREST

1:19 In Bible times, being betrothed meant the couple was legally promised to each other, but the bride didn't live with the bridegroom. After the wedding ceremony, the bride's family would have a big feast that lasted for six or seven days. Then the bride would go to live in her husband's house.

The Birth of John the Baptist

Zechariah and Elizabeth became the parents of John, just as the angel Gabriel had told Zechariah. Their son became the prophet who later announced the great news of the Messiah to the people of Israel and prepared them for Jesus' coming.

Luke 1:57–80

The Birth of John the Baptist

[57]When it was time for Elizabeth to have her baby, she gave birth to a son. [58]Her neighbors and relatives heard that the Lord had shown her great mercy, and they shared her joy.

[59]On the eighth day they came to circumcise the child, and they were going to name him after his father Zechariah, [60]but his mother spoke up and said, "No! He is to be called John."

[61]They said to her, "There is no one among your relatives who has that name."

[62]Then they made signs to his father, to find out what he would like to name the child. [63]He asked for a writing tablet, and to everyone's astonishment he wrote, "His name is John." [64]Immediately his mouth was opened and his tongue was loosed, and he began to speak, praising God. [65]The neighbors were all filled with awe, and throughout the hill country of Judea people were talking about all these things. [66]Everyone who heard this wondered about it, asking, "What then is this child going to be?" For the Lord's hand was with him.

Zechariah's Song

⁶⁷His father Zechariah was filled with the Holy Spirit and prophesied:

⁶⁸"Praise be to the Lord, the God of Israel,
>   because he has come and has redeemed his people.
⁶⁹He has raised up a horn*a* of salvation for us
>   in the house of his servant David
⁷⁰(as he said through his holy prophets of long ago),
⁷¹salvation from our enemies
>   and from the hand of all who hate us—
⁷²to show mercy to our fathers
>   and to remember his holy covenant,
⁷³   the oath he swore to our father Abraham:
⁷⁴to rescue us from the hand of our enemies,
>   and to enable us to serve him without fear
⁷⁵   in holiness and righteousness before him all our days.

⁷⁶And you, my child, will be called a prophet of the Most High;
>   for you will go on before the Lord to prepare the way for him,
⁷⁷to give his people the knowledge of salvation
>   through the forgiveness of their sins,
⁷⁸because of the tender mercy of our God,
>   by which the rising sun will come to us from heaven
⁷⁹to shine on those living in darkness
>   and in the shadow of death,
>   to guide our feet into the path of peace."

⁸⁰And the child grew and became strong in spirit; and he lived in the desert until he appeared publicly to Israel.

---

a 69 Horn here symbolizes strength.

1. What name did the people want Elizabeth to give her son? Why? (v. 59)
2. How was the baby's name finally chosen? (v. 63)
3. What happened to Zechariah when he wrote down the baby's name? (v. 64)

LET'S TALK

1. Names were very important during Bible times. They often told what the child meant to the parents or described who he or she would become. Why did your parents give you the name you have? Discuss the names of the people in your family and what they mean.
2. What do you suppose the people were actually saying when they were "talking about all these things" (v. 65)? What would you have talked about if you had heard something like this?

WHY THIS MATTERS

This story shows how much God loves us. He made sure that everything was ready for Jesus' birth by sending a messenger, John. God kept every promise he made and did the "impossible" to make it all happen just as he had said.

POINTS OF INTEREST

1:60 In Bible times, the mother often named a child. In the Old Testament, Leah, Rachel and Hannah named their children. A few times, someone else named a child: Pharaoh's daughter named Moses and the village women named Ruth's child Obed. Occasionally the father named a child or changed the name after the mother had selected one. That's why the people asked Zechariah what name he wanted for his son. He confirmed that the name of his son was John.

The Birth of Jesus

God had promised the people of Israel a Savior. Through the prophets, God had told them how the Savior would come and what he would do. All the things the prophets had said about Jesus' birth came to pass. Mary gave birth to Jesus in the town of Bethlehem, an ordinary, quiet place.

Luke 2:1–7

The Birth of Jesus

2 In those days Caesar Augustus issued a decree that a census should be taken of the entire Roman world. ²(This was the first census that took place while Quirinius was governor of Syria.) ³And everyone went to his own town to register.

⁴So Joseph also went up from the town of Nazareth in Galilee to Judea, to Bethlehem the town of David, because he belonged to the house and line of David. ⁵He went there to register with Mary, who was pledged to be married to him and was expecting a child. ⁶While they were there, the time came for the baby to be born, ⁷and she gave birth to her firstborn, a son. She wrapped him in cloths and placed him in a manger, because there was no room for them in the inn.

1. Why did Mary and Joseph go to Bethlehem? (vv. 1–3)
2. What was another name for the town of Bethlehem? (v. 4)
3. Why did Mary put the baby in a manger? (v. 7)

LET'S TALK

1. Can you think of some of the prophecies that were fulfilled when Jesus was born? Look back to the previous readings if you need to.
2. Why would God want his Son to be born in such a poor and ordinary place?

WHY THIS MATTERS

That night in Bethlehem, God came down to earth in the form of a little baby. God gave Jesus a humble beginning so that everyone could understand that he came to bring salvation to all people, even the poorest and lowliest. Jesus was born human, like us, so we could relate to him. He was God so that he could save us from our sins and give us new life.

POINTS OF INTEREST

2:7 The manger Mary laid Jesus in was a trough or open box used to hold grain or grasses to feed livestock. The area around Bethlehem has many limestone caves that were used in Bible times to shelter and feed animals. Although we think of a stable as a wooden building, the stable Jesus was born in may have been a cave located behind an inn.

The Shepherds and the Angels

Bethlehem was ordinarily a quiet town. But on the night that Jesus was born there, something happened outside of town — something spectacular!

Luke 2:8-20

The Shepherds and the Angels

[8] And there were shepherds living out in the fields nearby, keeping watch over their flocks at night. [9] An angel of the Lord appeared to them, and the glory of the Lord shone around them, and they were terrified. [10] But the angel said to them, "Do not be afraid. I bring you good news of great joy that will be for all the people. [11] Today in the town of David a Savior has been born to you; he is Christ[a] the Lord. [12] This will be a sign to you: You will find a baby wrapped in cloths and lying in a manger."

[13] Suddenly a great company of the heavenly host appeared with the angel, praising God and saying,

[14] "Glory to God in the highest,
    and on earth peace to men on whom his favor
        rests."

[15] When the angels had left them and gone into heaven, the shepherds said to one another, "Let's go to Bethlehem and see this thing that has happened, which the Lord has told us about."

[a] 11 Or *Messiah*. "The Christ" (Greek) and "the Messiah" (Hebrew) both mean "the Anointed One"; also in verse 26.

[16]So they hurried off and found Mary and Joseph, and the baby, who was lying in the manger. [17]When they had seen him, they spread the word concerning what had been told them about this child, [18]and all who heard it were amazed at what the shepherds said to them. [19]But Mary treasured up all these things and pondered them in her heart. [20]The shepherds returned, glorifying and praising God for all the things they had heard and seen, which were just as they had been told.

JUST THE FACTS

1. Who appeared to the shepherds out in the fields? (v. 9)

2. What did he say? (vv. 10–11)

3. What happened after this angel made his announcement? (v. 13)

LET'S TALK

1. Why were the shepherds terrified to see the angel and "the glory of the Lord"? (v. 9) How would you feel if you were camping out and saw this phenomenon?

2. What did the shepherds do after they went to see Jesus in the manger? Why?

WHY THIS MATTERS

The story of Jesus' birth had to be told, and the shepherds became witnesses to the indescribable miracle of the Messiah's coming. This story has amazed people for centuries, just as it amazed the shepherds and the people they told.

POINTS OF INTEREST

2:14 The hymn of the angels is called the "*Gloria in Excelsis Deo*," which is the refrain of the song "Angels We Have Heard on High" that we sing during the Christmas season. The phrase "Glory to God" praises the majesty of God, who dwells "in the highest" in heaven.

Mary and Joseph Present Jesus at the Temple

Forty days after his birth, Mary and Joseph took Jesus to the temple in Jerusalem. They were obeying religious laws that Moses had given the Israelites long before. They went to dedicate their firstborn son to God and to offer sacrifices.

Luke 2:21–40

Jesus Presented in the Temple

²¹ On the eighth day, when it was time to circumcise him, he was named Jesus, the name the angel had given him before he had been conceived.

²² When the time of their purification according to the Law of Moses had been completed, Joseph and Mary took him to Jerusalem to present him to the Lord ²³ (as it is written in the Law of the Lord, "Every firstborn male is to be consecrated to the Lord"[a]), ²⁴ and to offer a sacrifice in keeping with what is said in the Law of the Lord: "a pair of doves or two young pigeons."[b]

²⁵ Now there was a man in Jerusalem called Simeon, who was righteous and devout. He was waiting for the consolation of Israel, and the Holy Spirit was upon him. ²⁶ It had been revealed to him by the Holy Spirit that he would not die before he had seen the Lord's Christ. ²⁷ Moved by the Spirit, he went into the temple courts. When the parents brought in the child Jesus to do for

[a] 23 Exodus 13:2,12   [b] 24 Lev. 12:8

him what the custom of the Law required, ²⁸ Simeon took him in his arms and praised God, saying:

²⁹ "Sovereign Lord, as you have promised,
    you now dismiss[a] your servant in peace.
³⁰ For my eyes have seen your salvation,
³¹   which you have prepared in the sight of all
            people,
³² a light for revelation to the Gentiles
    and for glory to your people Israel."

³³ The child's father and mother marveled at what was said about him. ³⁴ Then Simeon blessed them and said to Mary, his mother: "This child is destined to cause the falling and rising of many in Israel, and to be a sign that will be spoken against, ³⁵ so that the thoughts of many hearts will be revealed. And a sword will pierce your own soul too."

³⁶ There was also a prophetess, Anna, the daughter of Phanuel, of the tribe of Asher. She was very old; she had lived with her husband seven years after her marriage, ³⁷ and then was a widow until she was eighty-four.[b] She never left the temple but worshiped night and day, fasting and praying. ³⁸ Coming up to them at that very moment, she gave thanks to God and spoke about the child to all who were looking forward to the redemption of Jerusalem.

³⁹ When Joseph and Mary had done everything required by the Law of the Lord, they returned to Galilee to their own town of Nazareth. ⁴⁰ And the child grew and became strong; he was filled with wisdom, and the grace of God was upon him.

[a] 29 Or *promised, / now dismiss*   [b] 37 Or *widow for eighty-four years*

1. Why did Mary and Joseph go to Jerusalem?
   (vv. 22–24)

2. How did Mary and Joseph react to what Simeon said?
   (v. 33)

3. How old was Anna? What did she do every day?
   (v. 37)

LET'S TALK

1. How did Simeon's blessing confirm who Jesus was?
   Why did Mary and Joseph marvel at what was said
   about their son?

2. What were Simeon and Anna waiting for? What kind
   of people were they?

WHY THIS MATTERS

Simeon and Anna were faithful people with hearts that
were open to God. Even though Jesus was very young, it
was clear to Simeon and Anna that he was the Messiah
the Jewish people had been waiting and hoping for.

POINTS OF INTEREST

2:24 To observe the Law of Moses, a woman who had
given birth to a son was to wait 40 days; then she was
to sacrifice a lamb and either a dove or a pigeon. If a
woman could not afford to bring a lamb and a dove
or pigeon, she was allowed to bring two doves or two
pigeons.

The Visit of the Magi

Several months after Jesus was born, Magi (traditionally called wise men) came from the east to Jerusalem asking about a new king. First, they asked King Herod, who was a friend of the Roman rulers, where to find the one they were looking for. Then they traveled another five miles to the town where Jesus lived in order to find him.

Matthew 2:1–12

The Visit of the Magi

2 After Jesus was born in Bethlehem in Judea, during the time of King Herod, Magi[a] from the east came to Jerusalem ²and asked, "Where is the one who has been born king of the Jews? We saw his star in the east[b] and have come to worship him."

³When King Herod heard this he was disturbed, and all Jerusalem with him. ⁴When he had called together all the people's chief priests and teachers of the law, he asked them where the Christ[c] was to be born. ⁵"In Bethlehem in Judea," they replied, "for this is what the prophet has written:

⁶"'But you, Bethlehem, in the land of Judah,
    are by no means least among the rulers of
        Judah;
for out of you will come a ruler
    who will be the shepherd of my people Israel.'[d]"

---

[a] 1 Traditionally *Wise Men*   [b] 2 Or *star when it rose*
[c] 4 Or *Messiah*   [d] 6 Micah 5:2

[7] Then Herod called the Magi secretly and found out from them the exact time the star had appeared. [8] He sent them to Bethlehem and said, "Go and make a careful search for the child. As soon as you find him, report to me, so that I too may go and worship him."

[9] After they had heard the king, they went on their way, and the star they had seen in the east[a] went ahead of them until it stopped over the place where the child was. [10] When they saw the star, they were overjoyed. [11] On coming to the house, they saw the child with his mother Mary, and they bowed down and worshiped him. Then they opened their treasures and presented him with gifts of gold and of incense and of myrrh. [12] And having been warned in a dream not to go back to Herod, they returned to their country by another route.

[a] 9 Or *seen when it rose*

JUST THE FACTS

1. Whom did the Magi say they were looking for? (v. 2)
2. What was the name of the king who was disturbed when he heard of another king being born? (v. 3)
3. What did the Magi do when they found Mary with her child? (v. 11)

LET'S TALK

1. Why was King Herod disturbed when he heard that the Messiah had been born? What did he think the Messiah would do?
2. Why do you think the Magi didn't go back to King Herod?

WHY THIS MATTERS

The Magi were the first to acknowledge Jesus as a king. This affirmed what the angel had said to Mary: Jesus would receive the throne of David, and his kingdom would have no end (see Luke 1:32–33).

POINTS OF INTEREST

2:2 Astronomers have explained that the star of Bethlehem was a comet, a nova or an alignment of Jupiter, Saturn and Mars. But history does not record that anyone besides the Magi saw this star. Apparently the star was a celestial phenomena God created just for this occasion.

Jesus, the Son of God, Is Baptized

When John grew up, he traveled from place to place telling people that the Messiah was coming and that they should change their ways. He did this to prepare them for the Messiah. Then he baptized them in the river to show that their hearts were clean. One day, Jesus came to be baptized too.

Matthew 3:13-17

The Baptism of Jesus

¹³Then Jesus came from Galilee to the Jordan to be baptized by John. ¹⁴But John tried to deter him, saying, "I need to be baptized by you, and do you come to me?"

¹⁵Jesus replied, "Let it be so now; it is proper for us to do this to fulfill all righteousness." Then John consented.

¹⁶As soon as Jesus was baptized, he went up out of the water. At that moment heaven was opened, and he saw the Spirit of God descending like a dove and lighting on him. ¹⁷And a voice from heaven said, "This is my Son, whom I love; with him I am well pleased."

JUST THE FACTS

1. What did John say to Jesus when Jesus came to be baptized? (v. 14)
2. What happened when Jesus came out of the water? (v. 16)
3. What did the voice from heaven say? (v. 17)

LET'S TALK

1. Jesus never sinned. So why did the Holy Spirit need to come down on him?
2. Why do you think it was important that God made this announcement?

WHY THIS MATTERS

The baptism of Jesus was the beginning of Jesus' work on earth. The Holy Spirit came down to give him the power to do miracles and heal people, to teach, and to do all the other things he came to do. God called Jesus his Son, encouraging him and announcing to everyone that he was the Messiah.

POINTS OF INTEREST

3:13 The Jordan River runs north to south from the Sea of Galilee to the Dead Sea. The distance between the two seas is 65 miles, but the Jordan, because it winds its way south, is actually 135 miles long. Before modern times, the Jordan was about 100 feet wide and three to ten feet deep, except when heavy rains in winter and spring caused it to flood.

From the Beginning

The Gospel of John tells us that the "word" is not only the spoken word (the message from God and Jesus' teachings) but also the "Word," Jesus, the actual person of God himself in Christ. He is the living expression of God's presence with his people.

John 1:1–18

The Word Became Flesh

1 In the beginning was the Word, and the Word was with God, and the Word was God. [2] He was with God in the beginning.

[3] Through him all things were made; without him nothing was made that has been made. [4] In him was life, and that life was the light of men. [5] The light shines in the darkness, but the darkness has not understood[a] it.

[6] There came a man who was sent from God; his name was John. [7] He came as a witness to testify concerning that light, so that through him all men might believe. [8] He himself was not the light; he came only as a witness to the light. [9] The true light that gives light to every man was coming into the world.[b]

[10] He was in the world, and though the world was made through him, the world did not recognize him. [11] He came to that which was his own, but his own did

---

[a] 5 Or *darkness, and the darkness has not overcome*   [b] 9 Or *This was the true light that gives light to every man who comes into the world*

not receive him. [12]Yet to all who received him, to those who believed in his name, he gave the right to become children of God— [13]children born not of natural descent,[a] nor of human decision or a husband's will, but born of God.

[14]The Word became flesh and made his dwelling among us. We have seen his glory, the glory of the One and Only,[b] who came from the Father, full of grace and truth.

[15]John testifies concerning him. He cries out, saying, "This was he of whom I said, 'He who comes after me has surpassed me because he was before me.'" [16]From the fullness of his grace we have all received one blessing after another. [17]For the law was given through Moses; grace and truth came through Jesus Christ. [18]No one has ever seen God, but God the One and Only,[b,c] who is at the Father's side, has made him known.

---

[a] 13 Greek *of bloods*   [b] 14 Or *the Only Begotten*   [c] 18 Some manuscripts *but the only* (or *only begotten*) *Son*

1. Who was in the beginning? (v. 1)
2. Whom did God send to tell about the "light"? (vv. 6–8)
3. What was given through Moses? What came through Christ? (v. 17)

LET'S TALK

1. What is grace? What are some of the blessings you have received because of God's grace?
2. What did the writer John mean by "darkness" and "light"? (vv. 4–5)

WHY THIS MATTERS

Long before the world began, God planned to send Jesus to live among people on earth. Through Jesus, God has shown us his glory.

POINTS OF INTEREST

1:4–5 Throughout the Bible, "light" is linked with God's majesty, glory and goodness, while "darkness" is linked with Satan and evil. John used these word pictures several times in this Gospel and in his letters.

God's Great Gift of Love

A Pharisee named Nicodemus came at night to ask Jesus who he was. Jesus told Nicodemus why he had come from God and what he was sent to do. Then Jesus told Nicodemus that Nicodemus would have to be "born again" of the Spirit. In a few sentences, Jesus summed up the Good News.

John 3:1–21

Jesus Teaches Nicodemus

3 Now there was a man of the Pharisees named Nicodemus, a member of the Jewish ruling council. [2] He came to Jesus at night and said, "Rabbi, we know you are a teacher who has come from God. For no one could perform the miraculous signs you are doing if God were not with him."

[3] In reply Jesus declared, "I tell you the truth, no one can see the kingdom of God unless he is born again.[a]"

[4] "How can a man be born when he is old?" Nicodemus asked. "Surely he cannot enter a second time into his mother's womb to be born!"

[5] Jesus answered, "I tell you the truth, no one can enter the kingdom of God unless he is born of water and the Spirit. [6] Flesh gives birth to flesh, but the Spirit[b] gives birth to spirit. [7] You should not be surprised at my saying, 'You[c] must be born again.' [8] The wind blows wherever it pleases. You hear its sound, but you cannot

[a] 3 Or *born from above*; also in verse 7   [b] 6 Or *but spirit*
[c] 7 The Greek is plural.

tell where it comes from or where it is going. So it is with everyone born of the Spirit."

[9] "How can this be?" Nicodemus asked.

[10] "You are Israel's teacher," said Jesus, "and do you not understand these things? [11] I tell you the truth, we speak of what we know, and we testify to what we have seen, but still you people do not accept our testimony. [12] I have spoken to you of earthly things and you do not believe; how then will you believe if I speak of heavenly things? [13] No one has ever gone into heaven except the one who came from heaven—the Son of Man.[a] [14] Just as Moses lifted up the snake in the desert, so the Son of Man must be lifted up, [15] that everyone who believes in him may have eternal life.[b]

[16] "For God so loved the world that he gave his one and only Son,[c] that whoever believes in him shall not perish but have eternal life. [17] For God did not send his Son into the world to condemn the world, but to save the world through him. [18] Whoever believes in him is not condemned, but whoever does not believe stands condemned already because he has not believed in the name of God's one and only Son.[d] [19] This is the verdict: Light has come into the world, but men loved darkness instead of light because their deeds were evil. [20] Everyone who does evil hates the light, and will not come into the light for fear that his deeds will be exposed. [21] But whoever lives by the truth comes into the light, so that it may be seen plainly that what he has done has been done through God."[e]

[a] 13 Some manuscripts *Man, who is in heaven*   [b] 15 Or *believes may have eternal life in him*   [c] 16 Or *his only begotten Son*
[d] 18 Or *God's only begotten Son*   [e] 21 Some interpreters end the quotation after verse 15.

1. What do people have to do in order to have eternal life? (v. 16)
2. Why did God send his Son into the world? (v. 17)
3. Why do people love the darkness more than the light? (vv. 19–20)

LET'S TALK

1. Verse 16 tells us what people have to do to have eternal life. What does it mean to "believe"? Why is this Good News so difficult for some people to understand?
2. What do we have to do to live by "the truth"? (v. 21) What does living by the truth look like?

WHY THIS MATTERS

The reason Jesus came to earth, lived and taught among people, and died for our sins is because "God so loved the world" (v. 16). Jesus is God's great gift of love to each and every one of us.

POINTS OF INTEREST

3:14 When Jesus talked about Moses lifting up the snake in the desert, he was referring to the time the Israelites complained about the food God had provided for them. God sent poisonous snakes into the camp to punish the people. Some people were saved from death by looking up at a bronze snake that God had told Moses to make and place on a pole.

Jesus Christ Is Supreme

Many years after Isaiah and Micah prophesied about Jesus the Messiah, the apostle Paul wrote a letter to the church at Colosse to tell them that Jesus was both God and a human being. Paul included this beautiful hymn in praise of the glory and supremacy of Christ.

Colossians 1:15–20

The Supremacy of Christ

[15] He is the image of the invisible God, the firstborn over all creation. [16] For by him all things were created: things in heaven and on earth, visible and invisible, whether thrones or powers or rulers or authorities; all things were created by him and for him. [17] He is before all things, and in him all things hold together. [18] And he is the head of the body, the church; he is the beginning and the firstborn from among the dead, so that in everything he might have the supremacy. [19] For God was pleased to have all his fullness dwell in him, [20] and through him to reconcile to himself all things, whether things on earth or things in heaven, by making peace through his blood, shed on the cross.

1. Paul said that Jesus Christ is the "firstborn." (v. 15) Of what is he the firstborn?
2. What did Jesus Christ create? (v. 16)
3. Of what is Jesus Christ the head? (v. 18)

LET'S TALK

1. What does it mean that Jesus Christ is the "image of the invisible God"? (v. 15)
2. What do you think Paul meant when he said that in Jesus Christ "all things hold together"? (v. 17)

WHY THIS MATTERS

Jesus was born in a small town and lived among common people like us, but Paul gives us the bigger picture of who Christ really is and what Christ has done for us.

POINTS OF INTEREST

1:19 In Paul's day, some people taught that matter — anything you could taste, see or touch — was evil, so the human body was evil. They said a person's spirit was "trapped" in an evil body and could escape only by some secret knowledge. So they said Jesus couldn't be both God and man because he lived in a body.

"Let All God's Angels Worship Him"

The author of the book of Hebrews, who did not identify himself, wrote this letter to Jewish Christians to encourage them in their faith. He reminded them that Jesus Christ came to the earth to fulfill the Old Testament Scriptures, that he is God, and that he is greater than even the angels.

Hebrews 1:1–14

The Son Superior to Angels

1 In the past God spoke to our forefathers through the prophets at many times and in various ways, ²but in these last days he has spoken to us by his Son, whom he appointed heir of all things, and through whom he made the universe. ³The Son is the radiance of God's glory and the exact representation of his being, sustaining all things by his powerful word. After he had provided purification for sins, he sat down at the right hand of the Majesty in heaven. ⁴So he became as much superior to the angels as the name he has inherited is superior to theirs.

⁵For to which of the angels did God ever say,

"You are my Son;
  today I have become your Father[a]"[b]?

Or again,

"I will be his Father,
  and he will be my Son"[c]?

[a] 5 Or *have begotten you*   [b] 5 Psalm 2:7   [c] 5 2 Samuel 7:14; 1 Chron. 17:13

⁶And again, when God brings his firstborn into the world, he says,

"Let all God's angels worship him."^a

⁷In speaking of the angels he says,

"He makes his angels winds,
    his servants flames of fire."^b

⁸But about the Son he says,

"Your throne, O God, will last for ever and ever,
    and righteousness will be the scepter of your
        kingdom.
⁹You have loved righteousness and hated wickedness;
    therefore God, your God, has set you above
        your companions
by anointing you with the oil of joy."^c

¹⁰He also says,

"In the beginning, O Lord, you laid the
        foundations of the earth,
    and the heavens are the work of your hands.
¹¹They will perish, but you remain;
    they will all wear out like a garment.
¹²You will roll them up like a robe;
    like a garment they will be changed.
But you remain the same,
    and your years will never end."^d

¹³To which of the angels did God ever say,

"Sit at my right hand
until I make your enemies
    a footstool for your feet"^e?

¹⁴Are not all angels ministering spirits sent to serve those who will inherit salvation?

---

^a 6 Deut. 32:43 (see Dead Sea Scrolls and Septuagint)
^b 7 Psalm 104:4   ^c 9 Psalm 45:6,7   ^d 12 Psalm 102:25-27
^e 13 Psalm 110:1

JUST THE FACTS

1. How did God speak to "our forefathers"? How does God speak "in these last days"? (vv. 1–2)

2. Where does the Son now sit? (v. 3)

3. What tasks has God given the angels? (vv. 6–7,14)

LET'S TALK

1. What words and phrases show how Christ is greater than the angels?

2. How does this reading help you understand the "big picture" of Jesus' coming?

WHY THIS MATTERS

The Messiah's coming was foretold by the prophets. Jesus was born and lived and died as a human being. Now Jesus Christ holds a position of honor in heaven at the right hand of God.

POINTS OF INTEREST

1:5 The author of this letter quoted two Old Testament texts that his original readers would have been familiar with — Psalm 2:7 and 2 Samuel 7:14 — to prove that Jesus Christ is God's Son.

The Family Reading Bible

If you've enjoyed the Christmas Story, con-sider exploring the complete Bible with your entire family. *The Family Reading Bible* provides a roadmap full of insightful and engaging questions and fun facts designed for you—a Christian parent looking for a way to read and explore the Bible together with your kids. With three easy-to-use reading tracks to accommodate children of any age, *The NIV Family Reading Bible* will nurture your kids' interest in God's Word.

Hardcover Edition: 978-0-310-94196-5

Pick up a copy at your favorite bookstore or online!

Phaedra ...

Sarah ....

Sarah Kane was born in 1971. Her first play *Blasted* was produced at the Royal Court Theatre Upstairs in 1995. Her second play, *Phaedra's Love*, was produced at the Gate Theatre in 1996. In April 1998, *Cleansed* was produced at the Royal Court Theatre Downstairs and in September 1998, *Crave* was produced by Paines Plough and Bright Ltd at the Traverse Theatre, Edinburgh. Her last play, *4.48 Psychosis*, premiered at the Royal Court Jerwood Theatre Upstairs in June 2000. Her short film *Skin*, produced by British Screen/Channel Four, premiered in June 1997. Sarah Kane died in 1999.

Methuen Drama

Published by Methuen 2002

3 5 7 9 10 8 6 4 2

This edition first published in Great Britain in 2002 by
Methuen Publishing Ltd, 11-12 Buckingham Gate, London SW1E 6LB

Phaedra's Love first published in 1996 by Methuen,
copyright © 1996 Sarah Kane

Sarah Kane has asserted her rights under the Copyright, Designs and Patents
Act, 1988, to be identified as the author of this work.

Methuen Publishing Limited Reg. No. 3543167

A CIP catalogue record for this book
is available from the British Library

ISBN 0 413 77112 1

Typeset by Deltatype Ltd, Birkenhead
Printed and bound in Great Britain by
Cox and Wyman Ltd, Reading, Berkshire

Caution

Phaedra's Love

My grateful thanks to Vincent O'Connell, Mel Kenyon and New Dramatists (New York), without whose support I could not have written this play.

For Simon, Jo and Elana.
With love.

Phaedra's Love was first performed at the Gate Theatre, London, on 15 May 1996. The cast was as follows:

Hippolytus	Cas Harkins
Phaedra	Philippa Williams
Strophe	Catherine Cusack
Doctor/Priest/Theseus	Andrew Maud
Man 1	Giles Ward
Man 2	Paolo De Paola
Woman 1	Catherine Neal
Woman 2	Diana Penny
Policeman	Andrew Scott

Directed by Sarah Kane
Designed by Vian Curtis

Characters

Hippolytus	*Crowd including:*
Doctor	**Man 1**
Phaedra	**Woman 1**
Strophe	**Child**
Priest	**Woman 2**
Theseus	**Man 2**
	Policeman 1
	Policeman 2

Author's note

Punctuation is used to indicate delivery, not to conform to the rules of grammar.

A stroke (/) marks the point of interruption in overlapping dialogue.

Words in square brackets [ ] are not spoken, but have been included in the text to clarify meaning.

Stage directions in brackets ( ) function as lines.

Editor's note

This edition of *Phaedra's Love*, first reprinted in 2000, incorporates minor revisions made to the original text by Sarah Kane shortly before her death. It should therefore be regarded as the definitive version in all respects.

Scene One

A royal palace.

Hippolytus *sits in a darkened room watching television.*
He is sprawled on a sofa surrounded by expensive electronic toys,
empty crisp and sweet packets, and a scattering of used socks and
underwear.
He is eating a hamburger, his eyes fixed on the flickering light of a
Hollywood film.
He sniffs.
He feels a sneeze coming on and rubs his nose to stop it.
It still irritates him.
He looks around the room and picks up a sock.
He examines the sock carefully then blows his nose on it.
He throws the sock back on the floor and continues to eat the hamburger.
The film becomes particularly violent.
Hippolytus *watches impassively.*
He picks up another sock, examines it and discards it.
He picks up another, examines it and decides it's fine.
He puts his penis into the sock and masturbates until he comes without
a flicker of pleasure.
He takes off the sock and throws it on the floor.
He begins another hamburger.

Scene Two

Doctor He's depressed.

Phaedra I know.

Doctor He should change his diet. He can't live on
hamburgers and peanut butter.

Phaedra I know.

Doctor And wash his clothes occasionally. He smells.

Phaedra I know. I told you this.

Doctor   What does he do all day?

Phaedra   Sleep.

Doctor   When he gets up.

Phaedra   Watch films. And have sex.

Doctor   He goes out?

Phaedra   No. He phones people. They come round.
They have sex and leave.

Doctor   Women?

Phaedra   There's nothing gay about Hippolytus.

Doctor   He should tidy his room and get some exercise.

Phaedra   My mother could tell me this. I thought you might
help.

Doctor   He has to help himself.

Phaedra   How much do we pay you?

Doctor   There's nothing clinically wrong. If he stays in
bed till four he's bound to feel low. He needs a
hobby.

Phaedra   He's got hobbies.

Doctor   Does he have sex with you?

Phaedra   I'm sorry?

Doctor   Does he have sex with you?

Phaedra   I'm his stepmother. We are royal.

Doctor   I don't mean to be rude, but who are these people
he has sex with? Does he pay them?

Phaedra   I really don't know.

Doctor   He must pay them.

Phaedra   He's very popular.

Doctor   Why?

Phaedra   He's funny.

Doctor   Are you in love with him?

Phaedra   I'm married to his father.

Doctor   Does he have friends?

Phaedra   He's a prince.

Doctor   But does he have friends?

Phaedra   Why don't you ask him?

Doctor   I did. I'm asking you. Does he have friends?

Phaedra   Of course.

Doctor   Who?

Phaedra   Did you actually talk to him?

Doctor   He didn't say much.

Phaedra   I'm his friend. He talks to me.

Doctor   What about?

Phaedra   Everything.

Doctor   (*Looks at her.*)

Phaedra   We're very close.

Doctor   I see. And what do you think?

Phaedra   I think my son is ill. I think you should help. I think after six years training and thirty years experience the royal doctor should come up with something better than he has to lose weight.

Doctor   Who looks after things while your husband is away?

Phaedra   Me. My daughter.

Doctor   When is he coming back?

Phaedra   I've no idea.

Doctor   Are you still in love with him?

Phaedra   Of course. I haven't seen him since we married.

Doctor   You must be very lonely.

Phaedra   I have my children.

Doctor   Perhaps your son is missing his father.

Phaedra   I doubt it.

Doctor   Perhaps he's missing his real mother.

Phaedra   (*Looks at him.*)

Doctor   That's not a reflection on your abilities as a substitute, but there is, after all, no blood between you. I'm merely speculating.

Phaedra   Quite.

Doctor   Although he's a little old to be feeling orphaned.

Phaedra   I didn't ask you to speculate. I asked for a diagnosis. And treatment.

Doctor   He's bound to be feeling low, it's his birthday.

Phaedra   He's been like this for months.

Doctor   There's nothing wrong with him medically.

Phaedra   Medically?

Doctor   He's just very unpleasant. And therefore incurable. I'm sorry.

Phaedra   I don't know what to do.

Doctor   Get over him.

Scene Three

Strophe *is working.*
Phaedra *enters.*

Strophe Mother.

Phaedra Go away fuck off don't touch me don't talk to me stay with me.

Strophe What's wrong?

Phaedra Nothing. Nothing at all.

Strophe I can tell.

Phaedra Have you ever thought, thought your heart would break?

Strophe No.

Phaedra Wished you could cut open your chest tear it out to stop the pain?

Strophe That would kill you.

Phaedra This is killing me.

Strophe No. Just feels like it.

Phaedra A spear in my side, burning.

Strophe Hippolytus.

Phaedra (*Screams.*)

Strophe You're in love with him.

Phaedra (*Laughs hysterically.*) What are you talking about?

Strophe Obsessed.

Phaedra No.

Strophe (*Looks at her.*)

Phaedra Is it that obvious?

Strophe I'm your daughter.

Phaedra   Do you think he's attractive?

Strophe   I used to.

Phaedra   What changed?

Strophe   I got to know him.

Phaedra   You don't like him?

Strophe   Not particularly.

Phaedra   You don't like Hippolytus?

Strophe   No, not really.

Phaedra   Everyone likes Hippolytus.

Strophe   I live with him.

Phaedra   It's a big house.

Strophe   He's a big man.

Phaedra   You used to spend time together.

Strophe   He wore me out.

Phaedra   You tired of Hippolytus?

Strophe   He bores me.

Phaedra   Bores you?

Strophe   Shitless.

Phaedra   Why? Everyone likes him.

Strophe   I know.

Phaedra   I know what room he's in.

Strophe   He never moves.

Phaedra   Can feel him through the walls. Sense him. Feel his heartbeat from a mile.

Strophe   Why don't you have an affair, get your mind off him.

Phaedra   There's a thing between us, an awesome fucking thing, can you feel it? It burns. Meant to be. We were. Meant to be.

Strophe   No.

Phaedra   Brought together.

Strophe   He's twenty years younger than you.

Phaedra   Want to climb inside him work him out.

Strophe   This isn't healthy.

Phaedra   He's not my son.

Strophe   You're married to his father.

Phaedra   He won't come back, too busy being useless.

Strophe   Mother. If someone were to find out.

Phaedra   Can't deny something this big.

Strophe   He's not nice to people when he's slept with them. I've seen him.

Phaedra   Might help me get over him.

Strophe   Treats them like shit.

Phaedra   Can't switch this off. Can't crush it. Can't. Wake up with it, burning me. Think I'll crack open I want him so much. I talk to him. He talks to me, you know, we, we know each other very well, he tells me things, we're very close. About sex and how much it depresses him, and I know –

Strophe   Don't imagine you can cure him.

Phaedra   Know if it was someone who loved you, really loved you –

Strophe   He's poison.

Phaedra   Loved you till it burnt them –

Strophe   They do love him. Everyone loves him.
He despises them for it. You'd be no different.

Phaedra   You could feel such pleasure.

Strophe   Mother. It's me. Strophe, your daughter. Look at
me. Please. Forget this. For my sake.

Phaedra   Yours?

Strophe   You don't talk about anything else any more.
You don't work. He's all you care about, but you
don't see what he is.

Phaedra   I don't talk about him that often.

Strophe   No. Most of the time you're with him. Even
when you're not with him you're with him. And
just occasionally, when you remember that you
gave birth to me and not him, you tell me how
ill he is.

Phaedra   I'm worried about him.

Strophe   You've said. See a doctor.

Phaedra   He –

Strophe   For yourself, not him.

Phaedra   There's nothing wrong with me. I don't know
what to do.

Strophe   Stay away from him, go and join Theseus, fuck
someone else, whatever it takes.

Phaedra   I can't.

Strophe   You can have any man you want.

Phaedra   I want him.

Strophe   Except him.

Phaedra   Any man I want except the man I want.

Strophe   Have you ever fucked a man more than once?

Phaedra This is different.

Strophe Mother, this family –

Phaedra Oh I know.

Strophe If anyone were to find out.

Phaedra I know, I know.

Strophe It's the excuse they're all looking for.
We'd be torn apart on the streets.

Phaedra Yes, yes, no, you're right, yes.

Strophe Think of Theseus. Why you married him.

Phaedra I can't remember.

Strophe Then think of my father.

Phaedra I know.

Strophe What would he think?

Phaedra He'd –

Strophe Exactly. You can't do it. Can't even think of it.

Phaedra No.

Strophe He's a sexual disaster area.

Phaedra Yes, I –

Strophe No one must know. No one must know.

Phaedra You're right, I –

Strophe No one must know.

Phaedra No.

Strophe Not even Hippolytus.

Phaedra No.

Strophe What are you going to do?

Phaedra Get over him.

Scene Four

Hippolytus *is watching television with the sound very low.*
He is playing with a remote control car.
It whizzes around the room.
His gaze flits between the car and the television apparently getting pleasure from neither.
He eats from a large bag of assorted sweets on his lap.
Phaedra *enters carrying a number of wrapped presents.*
She stands for a few moments watching him.
He doesn't look at her.
Phaedra *comes further into the room.*
She puts the presents down and begins to tidy the room – she picks up socks and underwear and looks for somewhere to put them. There is nowhere, so she puts them back on the floor in a neat pile.
She picks up the empty crisp and sweet packets and puts them in the bin.
Hippolytus *watches the television throughout.*
Phaedra *moves to switch on a brighter light.*

Hippolytus   When was the last time you had a fuck?

Phaedra   That's not the sort of question you should ask your stepmother.

Hippolytus   Not Theseus, then. Don't suppose he's keeping it dry either.

Phaedra   I wish you'd call him father.

Hippolytus   Everyone wants a royal cock, I should know.

Phaedra   What are you watching?

Hippolytus   Or a royal cunt if that's your preference.

Phaedra   (*Doesn't respond.*)

Hippolytus   News. Another rape. Child murdered. War somewhere. Few thousand jobs gone. But none of this matters 'cause it's a royal birthday.

Phaedra   Why don't you riot like everyone else?

Hippolytus   I don't care.

Silence.
Hippolytus *plays with his car.*

Hippolytus   Are those for me? Course they're fucking for
me.

Phaedra   People brought them to the gate. I think they'd
like to have given them to you in person. Taken
photos.

Hippolytus   They're poor.

Phaedra   Yes, isn't it charming?

Hippolytus   It's revolting. (*He opens a present.*) What the
fuck am I going to do with a bagatelle?
What's this? (*He shakes a present.*) Letter
bomb. Get rid of this tat, give it to Oxfam,
I don't need it.

Phaedra   It's a token of their esteem.

Hippolytus   Less than last year.

Phaedra   Have you had a good birthday?

Hippolytus   Apart from some cunt scratching my motor.

Phaedra   You don't drive.

Hippolytus   Can't now, it's scratched. Token of their
contempt.

Silence.
Hippolytus *plays with his car.*

Phaedra   Who gave you that?

Hippolytus   Me. Only way of making sure I get what I
want. Wrapped it up and everything.

Silence apart from the TV and car.

Phaedra   What about you?

Hippolytus   What about me? Want a sweet?

Phaedra   I –
No. Thank you.
The last time you –
What you asked me.

Hippolytus   Had a fuck.

Phaedra   Yes.

Hippolytus   Don't know. Last time I went out. When was that?

Phaedra   Months ago.

Hippolytus   Really? No. Someone came round. Fat bird. Smelt funny. And I fucked a man in the garden.

Phaedra   A man?

Hippolytus   Think so. Looked like one but you can never be sure.

Silence.

Hippolytus   Hate me now?

Phaedra   Course not.

Silence.

Hippolytus   Where's my present, then?

Phaedra   I'm saving it.

Hippolytus   What, for next year?

Phaedra   No. I'll give it to you later.

Hippolytus   When?

Phaedra   Soon.

Hippolytus   Why not now?

Phaedra   Soon. I promise. Soon.

They look at each other in silence.
Hippolytus *looks away.*
He sniffs.
He picks up a sock and examines it.
He smells it.

Phaedra That's disgusting.

Hippolytus What is?

Phaedra Blowing your nose on your sock.

Hippolytus Only after I've checked I haven't cleaned my
cum up with it first. And I do have them
washed.
Before I wear them.

Silence.
Hippolytus *crashes the car into the wall.*

Hippolytus What is wrong with you?

Phaedra What do you mean?

Hippolytus I was born into this shit, you married it. Was
he a great shag? Fucking must have been.
Every man in the country is sniffing round your
cunt and you pick Theseus, man of the people,
what a wanker.

Phaedra You only ever talk to me about sex.

Hippolytus It's my main interest.

Phaedra I thought you hated it.

Hippolytus I hate people.

Phaedra They don't hate you.

Hippolytus No. They buy me bagatelles.

Phaedra I meant –

Hippolytus I know what you meant. You're right.
Women find me much more attractive since

I've become fat. They think I must have a secret.

(*He blows his nose on the sock and discards it.*)

I'm fat. I'm disgusting. I'm miserable. But I get lots of sex. Therefore . . . ?

Phaedra (*Doesn't respond.*)

Hippolytus Come on, Mother, work it out.

Phaedra Don't call me that.

Hippolytus Therefore. I must be very good at it. Yes?

Phaedra (*Doesn't respond.*)

Hippolytus Why shouldn't I call you mother, Mother? I thought that's what was required. One big happy family. The only popular royals ever. Or does it make you feel old?

Phaedra (*Doesn't respond.*)

Hippolytus Hate me now?

Phaedra Why do you want me to hate you?

Hippolytus I don't. But you will. In the end.

Phaedra Never.

Hippolytus They all do.

Phaedra Not me.

They stare at each other.
Hippolytus *looks away.*

Hippolytus Why don't you go and talk to Strophe, she's your child, I'm not. Why all this concern for me?

Phaedra I love you.

Silence.

Hippolytus Why?

Phaedra You're difficult. Moody, cynical, bitter, fat, decadent, spoilt. You stay in bed all day then watch TV all night, you crash around this house with sleep in your eyes and not a thought for anyone. You're in pain. I adore you.

Hippolytus Not very logical.

Phaedra Love isn't.

Hippolytus *and* **Phaedra** *look at each other in silence. He turns back to the television and car.*

Phaedra Have you ever thought about having sex with me?

Hippolytus I think about having sex with everyone.

Phaedra Would it make you happy?

Hippolytus That's not the word exactly.

Phaedra No, but –
Would you enjoy it?

Hippolytus No. I never do.

Phaedra Then why do it?

Hippolytus Life's too long.

Phaedra I think you'd enjoy it. With me.

Hippolytus Some people do, I suppose. Enjoy that stuff. Have a life.

Phaedra You've got a life.

Hippolytus No. Filling up time. Waiting.

Phaedra For what?

Hippolytus Don't know. Something to happen.

Phaedra This is happening.

Hippolytus   Never does.

Phaedra   Now.

Hippolytus   Till then. Fill it up with tat. Bric-a-brac, bits and bobs, getting by, Christ Almighty wept.

Phaedra   Fill it up with me.

Hippolytus   Some people have it. They're not marking time, they're living. Happy. With a lover. Hate them.

Phaedra   Why?

Hippolytus   Getting dark thank Christ day's nearly over.

A long silence.

Hippolytus   If we fuck we'll never talk again.

Phaedra   I'm not like that.

Hippolytus   I am.

Phaedra   I'm not.

Hippolytus   Course you are.

They stare at each other.

Phaedra   I'm in love with you.

Hippolytus   Why?

Phaedra   You thrill me.

Silence.

Phaedra   Would you like your present now?

Hippolytus   (*Looks at her. Then turns back to the TV.*)

Silence.

Phaedra   I don't know what to do.

Hippolytus   Go away. It's obviously the only thing to do.

They both stare at the television.
Eventually, **Phaedra** *moves over to* **Hippolytus.**
He doesn't look at her.
She undoes his trousers and performs oral sex on him.
He watches the screen throughout and eats his sweets.
As he is about to come he makes a sound.
Phaedra *begins to move her head away — he holds it down and comes in her mouth without taking his eyes off the television.*
He releases her head.
Phaedra *sits up and looks at the television.*
A long silence, broken only by the rustling of **Hippolytus'** *sweet bag.*
Phaedra *cries.*

Hippolytus   There. Mystery over.

Silence.

Phaedra   Will you get jealous?

Hippolytus   Of what?

Phaedra   When your father comes back.

Hippolytus   What's it got to do with me?

Phaedra   I've never been unfaithful before.

Hippolytus   That much was obvious.

Phaedra   I'm sorry.

Hippolytus   I've had worse.

Phaedra   I did it because I'm in love with you.

Hippolytus   Don't be. I don't like it.

Phaedra   I want this to happen again.

Hippolytus   No you don't.

Phaedra   I do.

Hippolytus   What for?

Phaedra   Pleasure?

Hippolytus You enjoyed that?

Phaedra I want to be with you.

Hippolytus But did you enjoy it?

Phaedra (*Doesn't respond.*)

Hippolytus No. You hate it as much as me if only you'd admit it.

Phaedra I wanted to see your face when you came.

Hippolytus Why?

Phaedra I'd like to see you lose yourself.

Hippolytus It's not a pleasant sight.

Phaedra Why, what do you look like?

Hippolytus Every other stupid fucker.

Phaedra I love you.

Hippolytus No.

Phaedra So much.

Hippolytus Don't even know me.

Phaedra I want you to make me come.

Hippolytus Can't stand post-coital chats.
There's never anything to say.

Phaedra I want you –

Hippolytus This isn't about me.

Phaedra I do.

Hippolytus Fuck someone else imagine it's me. Shouldn't be difficult, everyone looks the same when they come.

Phaedra Not when they burn you.

Hippolytus No one burns me.

Phaedra   What about that woman?

Silence.
Hippolytus *looks at her.*

Hippolytus   What?

Phaedra   Lena, weren't you –

Hippolytus   (*Grabs* **Phaedra** *by the throat.*)

Don't ever mention her again.
Don't say her name to me, don't refer to
her, don't even think about her, understand?
Understand?

Phaedra   (*Nods.*)

Hippolytus   No one burns me, no one fucking touches me.
So don't try.

He releases her.
Silence.

Phaedra   Why do you have sex if you hate it so much?

Hippolytus   I'm bored.

Phaedra   I thought you were supposed to be good at it.
Is everyone this disappointed?

Hippolytus   Not when I try.

Phaedra   When do you try?

Hippolytus   Don't any more.

Phaedra   Why not?

Hippolytus   It's boring.

Phaedra   You're just like your father.

Hippolytus   That's what your daughter said.

A beat, then **Phaedra** *slaps him around the face as hard as*
she can.

Hippolytus   She's less passionate but more practised.
I go for technique every time.

Phaedra   Did you make her come?

Hippolytus   Yes.

Phaedra   (*Opens her mouth to speak. She can't.*)

Hippolytus   It's dead now. Face it. Can't happen again.

Phaedra   Why not?

Hippolytus   Wouldn't be about me. Never was.

Phaedra   You can't stop me loving you.

Hippolytus   Can.

Phaedra   No. You're alive.

Hippolytus   Wake up.

Phaedra   You burn me.

Hippolytus   Now you've had me, fuck someone else.

Silence.

Phaedra   Will I see you again?

Hippolytus   You know where I am.

Silence.

Hippolytus   Do I get my present now?

Phaedra   (*Opens her mouth but is momentarily lost for words.
Then.*)

You're a heartless bastard.

Hippolytus   Exactly.

Phaedra *begins to leave.*

Hippolytus   Phaedra.

Phaedra   (*Looks at him.*)

Hippolytus   See a doctor. I've got gonorrhoea.

Phaedra   (*Opens her mouth. No sound comes out.*)

Hippolytus   Hate me now?

Phaedra   (*Tries to speak. A long silence. Eventually.*)

No. Why do you hate me?

Hippolytus   Because you hate yourself.

Phaedra *leaves.*

Scene Five

Hippolytus *is standing in front of a mirror with his tongue out.*
Strophe *enters.*

Strophe   Hide.

Hippolytus   Green tongue.

Strophe   Hide, idiot.

Hippolytus *turns to her and shows her his tongue.*

Hippolytus   Fucking moss. Inch of pleurococcus on my
tongue. Looks like the top of a wall.

Strophe   Hippolytus.

Hippolytus   Showed it to a bloke in the bogs, still wanted to
shag me.

Strophe   Have you looked out the window?

Hippolytus   Major halitosis.

Strophe   Look.

Hippolytus   Haven't seen you for ages, how are you?

Strophe   Burning.

Hippolytus   You'd never know we live in the same
house.

Strophe   For fuck's sake, hide.

Hippolytus   Why, what have I done?

Strophe   My mother's accusing you of rape.

Hippolytus   She is? How exciting.

Strophe   This isn't a joke.

Hippolytus   I'm sure.

Strophe   Did you do it?

Hippolytus   What?

Strophe   Did you rape her?

Hippolytus   I don't know. What does that mean?

Strophe   Did you have sex with her?

Hippolytus   Ah. Got you.
Does it matter?

Strophe   Does it *matter*?

Hippolytus   Does it matter.

Strophe   Yes.

Hippolytus   Why?

Strophe   *Why*?

Hippolytus   Yes, why, I do wish you wouldn't repeat
everything I say, why?

Strophe   She's my mother.

Hippolytus   So?

Strophe   My mother says she was raped.
She says you raped her.
I want to know if you had sex with my mother.

Hippolytus   Because she's your mother or because of what
people will say?

Strophe   Because she's my mother.

Hippolytus   Because you still want me or because you want to know if she was better than you?

Strophe   Because she's my mother.

Hippolytus   Because she's your mother.

Strophe   Did you have sex with her?

Hippolytus   I don't think so.

Strophe   Was there any sexual contact between you and my mother?

Hippolytus   Sexual contact?

Strophe   You know exactly what I mean.

Hippolytus   Don't get stroppy, Strophe.

Strophe   Did she want to do it?

Hippolytus   You should have been a lawyer.

Strophe   Did you make her?

Hippolytus   You're wasted as a pseudo-princess.

Strophe   Did you force her?

Hippolytus   Did I force you?

Strophe   There aren't words for what you did to me.

Hippolytus   Then perhaps rape is the best she can do. Me. A rapist. Things are looking up.

Strophe   Hippolytus.

Hippolytus   At the very least it's not boring.

Strophe   You'll be lynched for this.

Hippolytus   Do you think?

Strophe   If you did it I'll help them.

Hippolytus   Of course. Not my sister after all. One of my victims.

Strophe   If you didn't I'll stand by you.

Hippolytus   A rapist?

Strophe   Burn with you.

Hippolytus   Why?

Strophe   Sake of the family.

Hippolytus   Ah.

Strophe   You're my brother.

Hippolytus   No I'm not.

Strophe   To me.

Hippolytus   Strange. The one person in this family who has no claim to its history is the most sickeningly loyal. Poor relation who wants to be what she never will.

Strophe   I'll die for this family.

Hippolytus   Yes. You probably will.
I told her about us.

Strophe   You what?

Hippolytus   Yes. And I mentioned that you'd had her husband.

Strophe   No.

Hippolytus   I didn't say you fucked him on their wedding night, but since he left the day after –

Strophe   Mother.

Hippolytus   A rapist. Better than a fat boy who fucks.

Strophe   You're smiling.

Hippolytus   I am.

Strophe   You're a heartless bastard, you know that?

Hippolytus   It's been said.

Strophe   This is your fault.

Hippolytus   Of course.

Strophe   She was my mother, Hippolytus, my mother.
What did you do to her?

Hippolytus   (*Looks at her.*)

Strophe   She's dead you fucking bastard.

Hippolytus   Don't be stupid.

Strophe   Yes.
What did you do to her, what did you fucking do?

    Strophe *batters him about the head.*
    Hippolytus *catches her arms and holds her so she can't hit him.*
    Strophe *sobs, then breaks down and cries, then wails*
    uncontrollably.

Strophe   What have I done? What have I done?

    Hippolytus' *hold turns into an embrace.*

Hippolytus   Wasn't you, Strophe, you're not to blame.

Strophe   Never even told her I loved her.

Hippolytus   She knew.

Strophe   No.

Hippolytus   She was your mother.

Strophe   She –

Hippolytus   She knew, she knew, she loved you.
Nothing to blame yourself for.

Strophe   You told her about us.

Hippolytus   Then blame me.

Strophe You told her about Theseus.

Hippolytus Yes. Blame me.

Strophe You –

Hippolytus Me. Blame me.

A long silence.
Hippolytus *and* **Strophe** *hold each other.*

Hippolytus What happened?

Strophe Hung.

Silence.

Strophe Note saying you'd raped her.

A long silence.

Hippolytus She shouldn't have taken it so seriously.

Strophe She loved you.

Hippolytus (*Looks at her.*) Did she?

Strophe Tell me you didn't rape her.

Hippolytus Love me?

Strophe Tell me you didn't do it.

Hippolytus She says I did and she's dead. Believe her.
Easier all round.

Strophe What is wrong with you?

Hippolytus This is her present to me.

Strophe What?

Hippolytus Not many people get a chance like this.
This isn't tat. This isn't bric-a-brac.

Strophe Deny it. There's a riot.

Hippolytus Life at last.

Strophe Burning down the palace. You have to deny it.

Hippolytus   Are you insane? She died doing this for me. I'm doomed.

Strophe   Deny it.

Hippolytus   Absolutely fucking doomed.

Strophe   For me. Deny it.

Hippolytus   No.

Strophe   You're not a rapist. I can't believe that.

Hippolytus   Me neither.

Strophe   Please.

Hippolytus   Fucked. Finished.

Strophe   I'll help you hide.

Hippolytus   She really did love me.

Strophe   You didn't do it.

Hippolytus   Bless her.

Strophe   Did you?

Hippolytus   No. I didn't.

He begins to leave.

Strophe   Where are you going?

Hippolytus   I'm turning myself in.

He leaves.
Strophe *sits alone for a few moments, thinking.*
She gets up and follows him.

Scene Six

A prison cell.

Hippolytus *sits alone.*
A **Priest** *enters.*

Priest   My son.

Hippolytus   Bit of a come down. Always suspected the world didn't smell of fresh paint and flowers.

Priest   I may be able to help you.

Hippolytus   Smells of piss and human sweat. Most unpleasant.

Priest   Son.

Hippolytus   You're not my father. He won't be visiting.

Priest   Is there anything you need?

Hippolytus   Got a single cell.

Priest   I can help you.

Hippolytus   Don't need tat.

Priest   Spiritually.

Hippolytus   Beyond that.

Priest   No one is beyond redemption.

Hippolytus   Nothing to confess.

Priest   Your sister told us.

Hippolytus   Us?

Priest   She explained the situation to me.

Hippolytus   She's not my sister.
Admit, yes. Confess, no.
I admit it. The rape. I did it.

Priest   Do you feel remorse?

Hippolytus   Will you be giving evidence?

Priest   That depends.

Hippolytus   No. No remorse. Joy, in fact.

Priest   At your mother's death?

Hippolytus   Suicide, not death. She wasn't my mother.

Priest   You feel joy at your stepmother's suicide?

Hippolytus   No. She was human.

Priest   So where do you find your joy?

Hippolytus   Within.

Priest   I find that hard to believe.

Hippolytus   Course you do. You think life has no
meaning unless we have another person in it
to torture us.

Priest   I have no one to torture me.

Hippolytus   You have the worst lover of all. Not only
does he think he's perfect, he is. I'm satisfied
to be alone.

Priest   Self-satisfaction is a contradiction in terms.

Hippolytus   I can rely on me. I never let me down.

Priest   True satisfaction comes from love.

Hippolytus   What when love dies? Alarm clock rings it's
time to wake up, what then?

Priest   Love never dies. It evolves.

Hippolytus   You're dangerous.

Priest   Into respect. Consideration.
Have you considered your family?

Hippolytus   What about it?

Priest   It's not an ordinary family.

Hippolytus   No. None of us are related to each other.

Priest   Royalty is chosen. Because you are more privileged
than most you are also more culpable. God –

Hippolytus There is no God. There is. No God.

Priest Perhaps you'll find there is. And what will you do then? There's no repentance in the next life, only in this one.

Hippolytus What do you suggest, a last minute conversion just in case? Die as if there is a God, knowing that there isn't? No. If there is a God, I'd like to look him in the face knowing I'd died as I'd lived. In conscious sin.

Priest Hippolytus.

Hippolytus I'm sure God would be intelligent enough to see through any eleventh hour confession of mine.

Priest Do you know what the unforgivable sin is?

Hippolytus Of course.

Priest You are in danger of committing it. It's not just your soul at stake, it's the future of your family –

Hippolytus Ah.

Priest Your country.

Hippolytus Why do I always forget this?

Priest Your sexual indiscretions are of no interest to anyone. But the stability of the nation's morals is. You are a guardian of those morals. You will answer to God for the collapse of the country you and your family lead.

Hippolytus I'm not responsible.

Priest Then deny the rape. And confess that sin. Now.

Hippolytus Before I've committed it?

Priest Too late after.

Hippolytus   Yes. The nature of the sin precludes
confession.
I couldn't confess if I wanted to.
I don't want to. That's the sin. Correct?

Priest   It's not too late.

Hippolytus   Correct.

Priest   God is merciful. He chose you.

Hippolytus   Bad choice.

Priest   Pray with me. Save yourself. And your country.
Don't commit that sin.

Hippolytus   What bothers you more, the destruction of
my soul or the end of my family? I'm not in
danger of committing the unforgivable sin. I
already have.

Priest   Don't say it.

Hippolytus   Fuck God. Fuck the monarchy.

Priest   Lord, look down on this man you chose, forgive his
sin which comes from the intelligence you blessed
him with.

Hippolytus   I can't sin against a God I don't believe in.

A long silence.

Priest   No.

Hippolytus   A non-existent God can't forgive.

Priest   No. You must forgive yourself.

Hippolytus   I've lived by honesty let me die by it.

Priest   If truth is your absolute you will die.
If life is your absolute –

Hippolytus   I've chosen my path. I'm fucking doomed.

Priest   No.

Hippolytus   Let me die.

Priest   No. Forgive yourself.

Hippolytus   (*Thinks hard.*)

I can't.

Priest   Why not?

Hippolytus   Do you believe in God?

Priest   (*Looks at him.*)

Hippolytus   I know what I am. And always will be. But you. You sin knowing you'll confess. Then you're forgiven. And then you start all over again. How do you dare mock a God so powerful? Unless you don't really believe.

Priest   This is your confession, not mine.

Hippolytus   Then why are you on your knees? God certainly is merciful. If I were him I'd despise you. I'd wipe you off the face of the earth for your dishonesty.

Priest   You're not God.

Hippolytus   No. A prince. God on earth. But not God. Fortunate for all concerned. I'd not allow you to sin knowing you'd confess and get away with it.

Priest   Heaven would be empty.

Hippolytus   A kingdom of honest men, honestly sinning. And death for those who try to cover their arse.

Priest   What do you think forgiveness is?

Hippolytus   It may be enough for you, but I have no intention of covering my arse. I killed a woman and I will be punished for it by

    hypocrites who I shall take down with me.
    May we burn in hell. God may be all powerful,
    but there's one thing he can't do.

Priest   There is a kind of purity in you.

Hippolytus   He can't make me good.

Priest   No.

Hippolytus   Last line of defence for the honest man.
    Free will is what distinguishes us from the
    animals.

    (*He undoes his trousers.*)

    And I have no intention of behaving like a
    fucking animal.

Priest   (*Performs oral sex on* **Hippolytus**.)

Hippolytus   Leave that to you.

    (*He comes.*
    He rests his hand on top of the **Priest**'s *head*.)

    Go.
    Confess.
    Before you burn.

Scene Seven

    Phaedra's *body lies on a funeral pyre, covered.*
    Theseus *enters.*
    He approaches the pyre.
    He lifts the cover and looks at **Phaedra**'s *face.*
    He lets the cover drop.
    He kneels by **Phaedra**'s *body.*
    He tears at his clothes, then skin, then hair, more and more
    frantically until he is exhausted.
    But he does not cry.
    He stands and lights the funeral pyre – **Phaedra** *goes up in*
    flames.

Theseus   I'll kill him.

Scene Eight

Outside the court.

A crowd of men, women and children has gathered, including **Theseus** *and* **Strophe***, both disguised.*

Theseus   Come far?

Man 1   Newcastle.

Woman 1   Brought the kids.

Child   And a barby. [barbecue]

Man 1   String him up, they should.

Woman 2   The bastard.

Man 1   Whole fucking pack of them.

Woman 1   Set an example.

Man 1   What do they take us for?

Woman 1   Parasites.

Man 2   We pay the raping bastard.

Man 1   No more.

Man 2   They're nothing special.

Woman 1   Raped his own mother.

Woman 2   The bastard.

Man 2   She was the only one had anything going for her.

Theseus   He'll walk.

Man 2   I'll be waiting at the fucking gate.

Man 1   Won't be the only one.

Woman 1   He's admitted it.

Strophe   That means nothing.

Woman 2   The bastard.

Theseus   Might go in his favour. Sorry your honour, reading my Bible every day, never do it again, case dismissed. Not going to lock a prince up, are they? Whatever he's done.

Man 2   That's right.

Man 1   No justice.

Theseus   Member of the royal family. Crown against the crown? They're not stupid.

Man 1   Pig-shit thick, the lot of them.

Man 2   She was all right.

Man 1   She's dead.

Theseus   You don't hang on to the crown for centuries without something between your ears.

Man 2   That's right.

Theseus   Show trial. Him in the dock, sacrifice the reputation of a minor prince, expel him from the family.

Man 2   Exactly, exactly.

Theseus   Say they've rid themselves of the corrupting element. But the monarchy remains intact.

Man 1   What shall we do?

Man 2   Justice for all.

Woman 1   He must die.

Man 2   Has to die.

Man 1   For our sake.

Man 2   And hers.

Woman 1   Don't deserve to live. I've got kids.

Man 1   We've all got kids.

Woman 1   You got kids?

Theseus   Not any more.

Woman 2   Poor bastard.

Man 2   Knows what we're talking about then, don't he.

Man 1   Scum should die.

Woman 1   Here he comes.

Woman 2   The bastard.

As **Hippolytus** *is taken past, the crowd scream abuse and hurl rocks.*

Woman 2   Bastard!

Man 1   Die, scum!

Woman 1   Rot in hell, bastard!

Man 2   Royal raping bastard!

Hippolytus *breaks free from the* **Policemen** *holding him and hurls himself into the crowd.*
He falls into the arms of **Theseus**.

Man 1   Kill him. Kill the royal slag.

Hippolytus *looks into* **Theseus**' *face.*

Hippolytus   You.

Theseus *hesitates, then kisses him full on the lips and pushes him into the arms of* **Man 2**.

Theseus   Kill him.

Man 2 *holds* **Hippolytus**.
Man 1 *takes a tie from around a child's neck and puts it around* **Hippolytus**' *throat. He strangles* **Hippolytus**, *who is kicked by*

the **Women** *as he chokes into semi-consciousness.*
Woman 2 *produces a knife.*

Strophe   No! No! Don't hurt him, don't kill him!

Man 2   Listen to her.

Man 1   Defending an in-bred.

Woman 1   What sort of a woman are you?

Theseus   Defending a rapist.

Theseus *pulls* **Strophe** *away from* **Woman 2** *who she is attacking.*
He rapes her.
The crowd watch and cheer.
When **Theseus** *has finished he cuts her throat.*

Strophe   Theseus.
Hippolytus.
Innocent.
Mother.
Oh, Mother.

She dies.
Man 1 *pulls down* **Hippolytus**' *trousers.*
Woman 2 *cuts off his genitals.*
They are thrown onto the barbecue.
The children cheer.
A child takes them off the barbecue and throws them at another child, who screams and runs away.
Much laughter.
Someone retrieves them and they are thrown to a dog.
Theseus *takes the knife.*
He cuts **Hippolytus** *from groin to chest.*
Hippolytus' *bowels are torn out and thrown onto the barbecue.*
He is kicked and stoned and spat on.
Hippolytus *looks at the body of* **Strophe**.

Hippolytus   Strophe.

Theseus   Strophe.

Theseus *looks closely at the woman he has raped and murdered.*
He recognises her with horror.
When **Hippolytus** *is completely motionless, the police who have*
been watching wade into the crowd, hitting them randomly.
The crowd disperses with the exception of **Theseus**.
Two **Policemen** *stand looking down at* **Hippolytus**.

Policeman 1   Poor bastard.

Policeman 2   You joking?

> (*He kicks* **Hippolytus** *hard.*)

> I've got two daughters.

Policeman 1   Should move him.

Policeman 2   Let him rot.

Policeman 2 *spits on* **Hippolytus.**
They leave.
Hippolytus *is motionless.*
Theseus *is sitting by* **Strophe**'s *body.*

Theseus   Hippolytus.
Son.
I never liked you.

> (*To* **Strophe**.)

> I'm sorry.
> Didn't know it was you.
> God forgive me I didn't know.
> If I'd known it was you I'd never have –

> (*To* **Hippolytus**.)

> You hear me, I didn't know.

Theseus *cuts his own throat and bleeds to death.*
The three bodies lie completely still.
Eventually, **Hippolytus** *opens his eyes and looks at the sky.*

Hippolytus   Vultures.

> (*He manages a smile.*)

If there could have been more moments
like this.

Hippolytus *dies.*
A vulture descends and begins to eat his body.